weekend houses

weekend houses

PENELOPE ROWLANDS ~ PHOTOGRAPHS BY MARK DARLEY

CHRONICLE BOOKS

SAN FRANCISCO

Text copyright © 2000 by Penelope Rowlands.
Photography copyright © 2000 by Mark Darley.
All rights reserved. No part of this book may be reproduced in any form
without written permission from the publisher.

Library of Congress Cataloging-in-Publication Data available.

ISBN 0-8118-2543-4

Printed in Hong Kong.

Designed by Design: M|W, New York

Several of the photographs in this book have previously appeared in the
following magazines: "Casa Cabernet," pp. 98, 99, 100, 102, in *Architectural
Digest*, March 2000; "A Woman's House," pp. 111, 113, 115, 116, 117, in
the *New York Times Magazine*, June 1999; "Dahlstrom House," on the cover and
pp. 133, 134, 135, *Coastal Living*, July 1998.

Distributed in Canada by Raincoast Books
9050 Shaughnessy Street
Vancouver, British Columbia V6P 6E5

10 9 8 7 6 5 4 3 2 1

Chronicle Books LLC
85 Second Street
San Francisco, California 94105

Web Site: www.chroniclebooks.com

To my mother, Arden James White, who loves
houses, and to Julian, my son

~ PENELOPE ROWLANDS

To my wife, stylist, and co-driver, Suzanne, and
our children, James and Miranda

~ MARK DARLEY

CONTENTS

INTRODUCTION

"... Happiness depends on leisure." ~ ARISTOTLE

Weekend houses. The very concept dates back at least to ancient Rome — a time when there were, literally, no weekends, at least as we calculate them today. Even so, the well-to-do would regularly retreat beyond city walls for a ritual change of scene. Almost everything has changed since those long-gone days, of course, but when it comes to the idea of decamping, of moving somewhere else on a regular basis, things are very much the same. Cities empty out, or at least some neighborhoods do, rhythmically, year in and year out. The ancient Romans escaped by means of horses and carriages; we pile into our station wagons, vans, and SUVs.

Why do we go? Because, quite simply, we have to get away. We can name a hundred reasons: the rush and manic energy of city life, murderous office politics, and nonstop social lives that feel like another form of work. But, in truth, it's something more. Much of the pleasure of going is to meet the people we become when we get there. Our weekend selves tend to be more easygoing, more curious, more outdoorsy, more fun. We're who we would be, all the time, if there were no business trips to prepare for, bosses to placate, or projects to complete. Or so we like to think.

The social critic Witold Rybczynski has described weekends as "temporary liberation." Happily, though, it's the kind of freedom that recurs. Come Monday morning we may be back at our weekday lives, but the beauty of the system is that Friday afternoon always looms ahead.

The houses in this book take many forms, almost as many as the people who dwell in them. They range from a contemporary rammed earth house to a timeworn adobe to a saltbox. What they have in common is a kind of underlying joy. Here, they seem to promise, your best moments will take place. Within their walls, we have more leisure time, time to delight in the world, in family and friends, in nature itself.

When photographer Mark Darley — my partner on this project — and I set out to create this book, we weren't necessarily looking for cutting-edge architecture or sumptuous interior design, although certainly here there are examples of both. What we were after, mainly, was style. Style is a funny thing, it turns out; it's both ephemeral (like love, you know it when it turns up) and pleasingly democratic. For, while it can certainly be bought — the world is full of great designers who see to that — it is also available for nothing to those who know where to look, an indelible lesson the legendary decorator Michael Taylor learned as a child, when he first appreciated the beauty of shells and other natural objects, things he would later add to his famous interiors.

Weekend homes, almost by definition, are more casual than the places where we spend most of our time. One couple whose retreat is shown here, architect Peter Wormser and his wife, Liz Milwe, deliberately kept their Connecticut seaside cottage spare, adding only some brightly painted furniture and beloved artworks by friends. Nearby, in upstate New York, interior designers Ron Wagner and Timothy Van Dam may have filled their neoclassical residence with antiques, but there's still a lot of whimsy present — including, in the formal dining room, a glass-fronted cabinet containing timeworn pottery shards, assorted Wedgwood pieces, and nests, feathers, and other natural objects — that might not have come so easily in a formal city apartment.

"It's not our main house, so we just kind of let him do his thing," one woman told me, describing the wide latitude she and her husband gave the Mexican architect Ricardo Legorreta when they commissioned him to create a house for them in Northern California's wine country. And this relaxed attitude recurs among all sorts of weekenders, whether a world-class architect is involved or not; in one way or another, almost everyone in this book said, or implied, something similar. "More whimsical things seem allowable here whereas they wouldn't be back home," is how Berta Shapiro, a Chicago-based interior designer, summed it up.

Shapiro's country house near Lake Michigan is a fine example of what weekend style is all about. There's nothing grand about this place; in fact, its origins could hardly be more humble. It started life as one of those log cabins that you order, in pieces, from a catalog then put together — as its original owners did — on your own. In her professional life, Shapiro has made a name for herself by designing interiors of all different styles, some of them formal, some even grand. But no such formality is in evidence here. Still, there is beauty everywhere: in the birdhouse collection, in the art (typically by Midwestern women) that graces the walls, and in numerous humble objects scattered about, from colorful pebbles to favorite art postcards.

There are plenty of other examples of weekend style within these pages, including the cabin where Paul Smith, a Wyoming hotel owner, retreats as often as he can to do as little as he can. When Mark and I first glimpsed this interior, in a photo album containing Smith family snapshots, we both reacted with delight. The obvious pleasure this owner took in his house, with its layer upon layer of Western artifacts and its utter lack of pretension, came through instantly. Across the country, a magnificent house in Southampton, New York, with interiors by the famous Manhattan interior designer Mario Buatta, could hardly be classified as informal, but it, too, projects essential weekend values: a porch on which to live as much as possible ("my daughter chases fireflies here," its owner told me); a rambling, fragrant garden in which to escape; a magnificent stretch of beach just down the road.

Sadly, one of our favorite places couldn't be included. The young Vancouver architects John and Patricia Patkau of Patkau Architects, Inc., have recently invented *La Petite Maison de Week-end*, a kind of minimalist machine for living, one that encapsulates, for us, the very concept of a part-time house. Entirely self-sufficient, it "can be located on any outdoor site where it will provide the basics for everyday life: shelter, sleeping loft, kitchen, shower, and composting toilet," as the Patkaus describe it. We'd planned to add this wondrous wood-and-steel structure as a kind of coda to our book — the ultimate weekend dwelling. But when the time came to track it down, this audacious creation was, inconveniently enough, sojourning somewhere else. Perhaps its sheer elusiveness — after all, how many houses just aren't home when you want to photograph them? — is somehow statement enough.

Maybe in the future we'll all be toting one of these inventions along behind our sleek electric vehicles, stopping for the weekend wherever we want to, whenever the urge strikes. But even if we aren't, even if we're still fighting our way down the Long Island Expressway to a retreat in Bridgehampton or cramming onto the last afternoon ferry to some windswept island off Maine, we'll be following an ancient craving: to make another life, perhaps a better one — quietly, temporarily — someplace else.

ON THE LAND

"The land was ours . . ."

The land has been everything to us for a very long time — for as long, in fact, as we humans have walked upon it. No wonder so many of us seek a way to ritually return to it. The weekend houses in this section aren't defined by their proximity to water or to vineyards or to mountain peaks. Stylistically, they're as varied as the people who dwell in them. There is architect Ross Anderson's utterly simple Vermont cabin, which, while incorporating many postmodern references, has its roots in the homespun New England vernacular. Or Puddin and Robert Clarke's adobe in the high-altitude hills of Santa Fe — a place of roaming coyotes and piñon forests that is still, amazingly enough, within city limits. If the Clarkes' cleverly restored dwelling seems to fit right into this landscape, it's probably because the adobe style developed, millennia ago, in just this sort of environment. Like the other houses in this section, this residence is closely integrated with the land. Whether that terrain is a generous-sized Wyoming ranch or a surprisingly green patch of New Mexico, it's really the same place: a bit of nature that we learn to love through the seasons, one that before too long becomes an inextricable part of us.

CHEYENNE, WYOMING.

WAGNER/VAN DAM FARMHOUSE

It's not everyone who, having found the perfect neoclassical weekend house, can fill it instantly with a couple of truckloads of antique furniture from the same era, but that's exactly what interior designers Timothy Van Dam and Ron Wagner did after they bought their twenty-five-hundred-square-foot house in Columbia County, just north of New York City. "We're inveterate collectors," explains Van Dam, who, with Wagner, is a principal in the New York design firm Wagner Van Dam Design & Decoration, which specializes in residential interiors. So filling the house was a snap.

The two had fallen in love with this part of the almost impossibly lush Hudson Valley years earlier ("It just struck a chord with us," Van Dam says), and set out to buy a house there, preferably one where little work was required. (Having put years of restoration into their upper Manhattan townhouse, they weren't in a rush to repeat the experience.) Then, one day, they came across their diminutive, yet perfect, neoclassical farmhouse, which dates from the first half of the nineteenth century, and never looked back. "We fell in love with all the details, down to the high ceilings and the wide-plank pine floors," Van Dam reports.

Little, happily, needed to be done. "We could just move in and start enjoying it," Van Dam says. They painted a few rooms, including the kitchen ("It was three shades of dark green," he recalls), changed a center island, and added crown molding to that room's reconfigured cabinetry. They also made some small structural changes — adding a closet, deleting a short corridor, fattening up some scrawny back-porch columns. The two loved the living room's rich ochre color and chose to keep it as is; after "Timothy, being a proper Dutchman, washed down the walls," as Wagner puts it, the room looked freshly painted.

Throughout the house, American furniture predominates: there's a magnificent American empire sofa (covered in rose-colored Scalamandré silk with embroidered Napoleonic bees) in the living room and, in the dining room, some early twentieth-century chairs in the style of T. H. Robsjohn-Gibbings. And there are numerous souvenirs of the outdoors. Sometimes both worlds collide, as in the American empire dining room cabinet that Van Dam calls "Professor Wagner's cabinet of natural curiosities." It's full of such natural wonders as turkey feathers, fragments of pottery, and a hornet's nest that once graced the side of the house. Also present are some contemporary pieces of Wagner's own design, including iron tortière tables in the dining room and a side table in the master bedroom.

One of this house's great lessons is that decorating beautifully doesn't need to cost a lot. The owners picked up one of the living room's key pieces, an eighteenth-century mirror of indeter-

From the pond, which was installed by the owners, the house reveals its classical lines. "It's a small house, but it has grand pretensions," says interior designer Timothy Van Dam, who is one of the house's co-owners.

"It's the best of both worlds," Ron Wagner says of this diminutive neoclassical farmhouse. "It's as solid as a new house, but it has all the charm and character of an old one."

OPPOSITE PAGE: Van Dam arranging flowers. His garden plan for the property is so ambitious that he jokingly equates it with the elaborate layouts at Versailles.

minate origin, at a local flea market, while the grandiose-looking bed in the master bedroom is artfully hung with curtains to resemble a four-poster bed. "It's a totally false bed," Wagner confesses.

As for the grounds, "We have a garden plan drawn up that looks a bit like Versailles," Van Dam says. The designers have done wonders with their twenty-four acres, expanding a pond and, in the beaux-arts tradition, creating a long, beautifully symmetric allée, in this case of indigenous sweet gum trees. "What we like about them is that they have a neoclassical leaf, which we thought was perfect," Wagner says.

The two weekend here, almost without fail, throughout the year, delighting in each change of season. They spend their days gardening — "We're outside from just about when we get up until evening," according to Van Dam — and shopping, both for themselves and clients, in nearby Hudson, New York, a town featuring some sixty-five antique shops. Their evenings revolve around friends. "We used to entertain a lot in the city. Now, we entertain people here," Wagner says. "The circle has shifted. Having a weekend house has truly changed our lives."

LEFT: A pair of sneakers brings an otherworldly interior sharply into the present. The master bedroom is painted in Sienna Rose. "It's trompe l'oeil," Van Dam says of the bed, which resembles a four poster.

TOP: This combined library and guest room was formerly a pantry off the kitchen.

TOP: As in the rest of the house, in the dining room, American empire pieces predominate. This period sofa, covered in its original horsehair, blends easily with chairs from the early twentieth century done in the style of T. H. Robsjohn-Gibbings.

BOTTOM: "It's all the natural history things we love," Van Dam says of the dining room's curio cabinet, another American empire piece. Among its treasures: parian busts of nineteenth-century writers and philosophers; nests from the property; a stuffed pheasant.

A neoclassical vision: Both the Grecian-style sofa and mahogany chest of drawers are American empire. The print recounting the story of Moses is by Alma-Tadema. The fabric is by Scalamandré.

TOP LEFT: Mantel detail. The designers discovered the antique round mirror at a garage sale. The urn is one of a pair of chestnut warmers and is made of tole. Both these and the brass candlesticks date from the early 1800s.

TOP RIGHT: In the living room, an opaline glass lamp casts light on a table covered in toile de Jouy (from Clarence House). The contemporary chandelier is empire style.

BOTTOM LEFT: The view to the combined den and guest bedroom. The columns on either side of the door are from the farmhouse where Van Dam grew up in rural Michigan.

SMITH CABIN

BUFORD, WYOMING

"I just happened onto it," Paul Smith says of his weekend place in Wyoming, just west of Cheyenne. One day, while trekking around the countryside in the shadow of Saddleback Hill, he came upon an unprepossessing 1950s-era wood cabin, complete with a collapsing porch ("It was falling apart"). But he loved the structure anyway, mainly for its verdant location: Remount Ranch, where the author Mary O'Hara wrote *My Friend Flicka, The Green Grass of Wyoming*, and other Western classics.

What followed was "not so much a renovation but a reconstruction," says Smith, who's a third-generation owner of a "very eclectic" two-hundred-sixty-room Cheyenne hotel called The Hitching Post. He hired a locally based Latvian wood craftsman to refurbish the twenty-five-hundred-square-foot, two-bedroom abode inside and out, adding wood paneling and even elevating the porch. As for its decor, he came up with "total cowboy with a mix of English." Sure, there's a good European antique or two (including, in the living room, a Georgian low table), but, both inside and out, it's the West that predominates.

Soon after he bought the place, Smith's passion for Western-style furniture flowered. He promptly acquired three pieces by Thomas Molesworth, a Cheyenne-based furniture maker who was active from the 1930s to the 1960s, for the now-laughable price of five hundred dollars. (Such pieces are "very, very collectible now," Smith says, adding that fans of Molesworth and his Shoshone Furniture Company are particularly legion in Hollywood, where they include studio head Michael Eisner.) Smith's first Molesworths — an aqua leather sofa and two matching armchairs, done in burled oak with bright Chimayo cushions — still take pride of place in the upstairs sitting room.

The rest is a colorful, eclectic mix. There's plenty more Molesworth, including several leather lamps, as well as an Arts and Crafts–type table that, with its side tacking, blends in surprisingly well with more Western furnishings. ("There's some definite relationship" between the two styles, Smith avers.) There are also seemingly

This Wyoming cabin was fully restored. On the porch, which was elevated in the renovation, a Chimayo blanket brightens a willow chair.
"I've always had some interest in Western furnishings, but I didn't really develop it until I purchased the cabin," says owner Paul Smith.

LEFT: The teepee, which was made in Cheyenne, doubles as a guest house. It's also used for entertaining, making music, and something Smith calls "ceremonial drinking."

RIGHT: Located in the flatlands about twenty miles west of Cheyenne, Smith's rustic cabin "has a 360-degree view of the world," he says. It's set on the 4,000-acre ranch where the quintessentially Western novel *My Friend Flicka* was written.

endless variations on a cowboy-and-Indians theme: stirrup lamps; a wonderfully ornate, 1950s-era gold cowboy clock; a contemporary teepee-shaped lamp bought in Jackson Hole; a vintage photo of a Native American by renowned photographer Thomas Curtis.

Smith is such an inveterate collector that he owns — and wears to special events, such as Cheyenne's annual Diamond and Denim Cattle Baron's Ball — some vintage suits, including a midnight blue tuxedo that once belonged to Gene Autry, the famous singing cowboy. Indeed, there are traces of assorted Western legends, including Roy Rogers and Dale Evans, all over the house. In the entryway, a

framed letter by Rogers — with the matchless salutation of "Howdy Partner!" — seems to sum up the laid-back cowboy style.

From its contents to its views, the cabin speaks, quintessentially, of the West. Smith comes to this exhilarating expanse of green each weekend for contemplation, as much as anything else. "It's definitely my place for quiet. I find myself, when I'm here, just doing a lot of gazing. Not just reading, but looking. The skies are amazing here." For all the work he's put into it, he insists that his cabin's most important quality is invisible to the eye. "One of the attractions is the spirituality of it," he says. "It's a very spiritual spot."

TOP: On the sunporch is a signed blue Molesworth chair with its original leather intact. The burled oak legs exemplify the Western furniture made by Thomas Molesworth, who was active between the 1930s and the 1960s.

BOTTOM: In the shadow of the sunporch, an ominous boulder looms. The lamp dates from the 1940s, although its shade was designed by a contemporary artist. The red curtains are Canadian, from Roots Home.

TOP: This classic Molesworth desk is made of peeled Wyoming wood and red leather. The stirrup lamp is from the 1950s; its photographic shade, while new, is "typical of the era," Smith says. The pine interior paneling was done by a local craftsman.

BOTTOM: In the entry hall, signed vintage photographs of Dale Evans and other Western stars vie for space with more natural regional souvenirs.

TOP: In the dining room, cowboyana runs rampant. The turquoise Molesworth chair came from a bank in Shoshoni, Wyoming. The 1940s-era buffalo china is from the Smith family hotel, The Hitching Post.

BOTTOM: Thomas Molesworth incorporated Chimayo blankets into many of his designs. His chairs with burled oak legs, such as these, are particularly prized. The striped Wilton weave carpet dates from the 1950s.

ANDERSON CABIN

NEWFANE, VERMONT

Architect Ross Anderson describes his Vermont weekend house as being on "the last chunk of land at the end of the last dirt road." Which is to say that it's demonically inaccessible, with a steep, rock-strewn driveway — or are they boulders? — that discourages even four-wheel-drive vehicles. It's hard not to speculate, as you make your way up the steep hill, whether in the case of this rustic retreat, described by Anderson as "the antidote to New York," the cure might not be worse than the disease.

But such thoughts vanish the minute you reach the house. The architect refers to his place, with clear affection, as "a shack" or "the hovel" but, in truth, neither term applies. There's nothing flimsy or slapdash about this serenely innovative six-hundred-fifty-square-foot structure, although it happened to be, for the first few years of its existence, both plumbing- and electricity-free. ("Minimal budget, no power" is how Anderson summed up the project's constraints.) Instead, it's a jewel of the north, one that is best appreciated at night, when (thanks to translucent fiberglass paneling, which alternates with opaque) indoor light shines through its facade in sharply etched horizontal lines. "It glows softly like a paper lantern in the woods," as the owner/architect puts it.

One of the first things Anderson did after buying his hundred acres was to put in a pond. "It made the place feel like a place. It became a destination," he says. There were also practical reasons for doing

so, since he planned to build his house himself: "I knew there'd be a lot of sweat equity. I thought it would be nice to be able to jump in."

The challenge, architecturally, was "how to make something that had some kinship to structures that preexist in the landscape." The architect loves Vermont and wanted a house that gave a nod to local agricultural building traditions, including corn cribs, which he likes for their relative transparence, and the tobacco barns that are characteristic of the Connecticut Valley. "They're very manipulable structures," he says of the latter. "I also loved the way they looked. They fit into the land."

His house does, too, beautifully. It juts out from a maple sugar grove, overlooking a forest on one side, a meadow on another. And Anderson and his wife, film producer Nina Santisi, really did build

Architect Ross Anderson's house was inspired, in part, by the classic white clapboard Vermont farmhouse. "I wanted to flip that and make a black building where you still read the horizontal lines," he says.

OPPOSITE PAGE ~ **TOP LEFT:** "The idea that this house is not about color seemed to make it sit in the ground better," Anderson says of his house's black-and-white facade.

TOP RIGHT: The house is divided in two, with one half containing the kitchen and sleeping areas; the other, a screened porch. Because only half of it is insulated, "the house in winter is a lot smaller," Anderson says.

BOTTOM: Summer weekends at this Vermont house center around its trout-filled man-made pond.

Fishing equipment is kept in the dog-trot breezeway, which functions as a mudroom. The family takes its meals there in the summer; in the winter, it's the dog's domain.

it themselves, completing it in less than two years, on a weekends-only basis, with the help of assorted friends and neighbors. Of the completed structure, he says: "It always reminded me of the classic Vermont farmhouse, painted white and made of horizontal clapboards. I wanted to flip that and make a black building, where you still read the horizontal lines."

You enter the house through a green-walled breezeway that's multipurpose with a vengeance, being a mudroom, occasional dining room, campsite for friends, and where "the dog hangs out," as Anderson puts it. To the left is the screened porch; to the right, a combined living and dining room, kitchen, and sleeping loft. The living area is furnished just as it should be: sparely. What counts is

the way the light, during the day, streams in through the facade for a basket-weave effect. (At night, light flows in the other direction, artfully illuminating the rural blackness.) Not to mention the windows, pine-clad ceilings, and potbellied stove, all of which telegraph the essence of Vermont.

Curiously, the cabin has changed the land, or rather the pond has, drawing ducks, herons, deer, and moose. Now well stocked with trout, it attracts weekend fishermen, too, including the couple's young daughter, Eva. Although the cabin is only three hours and change from the family's loft in SoHo, in lower Manhattan, it might as well be in another universe. And that's precisely the point.

LEFT: Until recently, when plumbing was installed, the cabin's bathroom looked like this, with no pipes anywhere and a metal bowl for a sink.

TOP RIGHT: The living and sleeping areas, as seen from the loft. The light fixture is by Wally Vogelsburg of Solebury Forge.

BOTTOM RIGHT: In summer, the screened porch becomes another room. "It's a way to get really into the landscape in a hurry," according to the architect.

OPPOSITE PAGE: The combined living room and kitchen, looking toward the sleeping loft. For transparence and added light, Anderson used layers of tinted green acrylic for part of its walls.

DANSON HOUSE

TESUQUE, NEW MEXICO

Almost everyone who goes to New Mexico seems to fall in love with the place, and Casey Danson, a Los Angeles–based environmental designer and activist, is no exception. "I basically started coming to Santa Fe about twelve years ago because it called me," she says. "I'd go every four or five weeks and come home just like a new person. It's powerful spiritually because of the whole convergence of mountains there. It has a strong spiritual force."

The seven-acre property in Tesuque, just north of Santa Fe, that Danson shares with her two daughters is a fertile patch of green in the otherwise arid-seeming Southwestern landscape. A well-known irrigation ditch, the Acequia Madre — "the ancient mother ditch," as Danson calls it — passes through her property, bringing with it lots of greenery and peaceful, streamlike sounds.

When Danson first came upon her house and land, both seemed gloomy. "It was an extremely unfriendly masculine house," she recalls. Its exposed terra cotta–colored adobe-style walls, without a plaster overlay, seemed hard edged. In addition, the building was surrounded on all sides by "black patios with huge four-by-four foot columns that blocked the view of meadows and fields, including the most beautiful willows and elder trees I've ever seen."

Also blighting the property were "hundreds of seven-ton stones," according to Danson, who says these were used by a previous owner for the celebration of solstices and other natural events. "They blocked the house in from any connection to the earth or view of the land. You couldn't even see the mountains."

Danson had the land cleared; as for the house itself, she expanded it by adding a master bedroom, passageway, and bath, along with a tiny back patio, bringing the total footage up to four thousand square feet. She brightened the dark exterior by adding pale color-coated plaster to the adobe walls and painting its gray roof tiles red. Inside, she had the dark brick floor replaced with one of light Colorado stone. She also added a two-bedroom guest house that is completely solar, in keeping with her professional interests

"It's where we live most," environmental designer Casey Danson says of this outdoor room, which replaced some unsightly patios. With its fireplace and generously proportioned willow furniture, this area, which she designed, is a favorite family gathering spot.

33

(Danson's firm, Global Possibilities, promotes the use of solar and sustainable forms of energy).

The property's most charming addition just may be the seventeen-by-twenty-one-foot outdoor room — "it's a living room, really," Danson says — where much of her family life takes place. "We have lunch and dinner in it, and we entertain. We sit out there in the winter with a fire in the outdoor fireplace. It's just a beautiful place to be." She also added a half-moon-shaped garden in front of the kitchen, "sort of like an altar facing the east."

Danson wanted a romantic, very feminine interior. "It's a very pink and red house, only for girls," she says with a laugh. From uphol-stery to artwork, much of the inside is conceived in these pale shades. She sculpted the figurative bronzes that dot the rooms herself. Other pieces here are mainly by local artists, including Dan Amingha, a well-regarded New Mexican painter of mixed Hopi-Tewa extraction. The stone carvings throughout were done by a Sioux medicine man named Stormy RedDoor.

Not long ago, Danson thought of selling the place, but it wasn't meant to be. "I was thinking of sizing down, but then I came out to the house," she recalls. "There was a purple sunset and the grasses were swaying and the birds were calling and I realized there's no way I could ever give this up. It's a very special place."

TOP: In the renovation of her New Mexican adobe-style house, Danson added French doors and replaced black brick floors with Colorado stone. The chaise longue is French provincial; the blanket, Mexican.

BOTTOM LEFT: In the study, a colonial Mexican bench and a painting by the late Santa Fe artist Susan Hertel. Danson wanted a feminine interior, and kept the color palette pale throughout.

BOTTOM RIGHT: Just beyond a guest bathroom, at the back of the house, flows the legendary Acequia Madre, the ancient irrigation ditch that, along with the nearby Tesuque Creek, keeps this part of Santa Fe green.

GOODMAN FARMHOUSE

NEAR BRATTLEBORO, VERMONT

"I wanted a house that reflected my life," says Lou Goodman, a New York architect and furniture designer who spends his weekends on a two-hundred-acre Vermont farm he describes as "a very serene, but very hardworking retreat." Here, relaxation hardly resembles leisure. First there's the five-hour drive up from Goodman's Greenwich Village apartment, which, on a week-in, week-out basis, seems like work enough. And then there's the never-ending task of maintaining this traditional New England farmhouse, with its assorted outbuildings and two hundred acres of land. (Not to mention the work that spills over from both Goodman's architectural practice and his teaching post at the Pratt Institute.)

He first came upon the place twenty years ago, when he was looking for a tranquil place to work. "I've been quietly renovating it ever since, the land as well as the house," Goodman explains. "It's been a process of cleaning up the outside, the buildings, the exterior walls, and the interiors." An avid gardener, he collaborated with a friend, Stephen Belliveau, on the property's beautiful gardens, some of which are geometric, others more fluid and meandering. The white garden was entirely designed by Belliveau; surrounded by white birch trees and full of hydrangeas, irises, and other flowers, it's a much-loved place to walk on bright moonlit nights.

Although he spends most of his time on architectural projects, Goodman also takes a keen interest in interior design. There's nothing discordant about the way he filled a nineteenth-century New England house with pieces that project a sharp-lined modernity; both the house and its contents — from local potter Richard Foye's ceramics to a spare, Goodman-designed dining table — share a purity of line, and are thus surprisingly compatible.

When he first moved in, the place was furnished with what Goodman calls "so-called antiques." Gradually, these have been supplanted by furniture of his own design, as well as the kind of modernist furniture, including a minimalist-looking highboy, that he sold at his Gallery of Applied Arts in Manhattan before it closed in 1990. (Other pieces, such as the 1950s-era curved sofa — a circular counterpoint to the room's right angles and sharply defined lines — came from Goodman's family.) He describes the furniture he designs as "minimal enough to be modern, shapely enough to be traditional, classic in character."

The same description could apply to his farmhouse. In keeping with his rural surroundings, Goodman tries "to keep the house as low-tech as possible." There's no television and, while the plumbing is perfectly adequate, this owner has been known to bypass the shower for the revivifying experience of soaking in a nearby stream. For Goodman, weekends here are a perfect way to recharge. "It's active. It's not like going away and having nothing to do," he says. "But what you do do is compelling, and that's restful. It takes you away from what you're doing in New York City."

Like so many New England houses, architect Lou Goodman's meticulously restored Vermont farmhouse, which dates from the mid-1800s, has been added to over the years. Guest quarters were added about a century later.

TOP: A view from the second floor shows the house's fine rustic detailing, including plaster walls and a painted wooden floor, in the style of old Vermont. The new mahogany-and-glass French doors were patterned after the house's original front door.

BOTTOM: Part of Goodman's eclectic pottery collection is displayed on a cherry chest of his own design. Shown here: African and cloisonné pieces. The blue Chinese vase came from an antique store in Vermont.

OPPOSITE PAGE: The owner designed the front hall's ebony-stained cherry table with frosted glass inset. The African sculpture, by a Masai warrior, is of the artist's own shadow.

TOP: In the dining room, a vase by local potter Richard Foye sits on a walnut dining table by Goodman. The chair fabric is by Jack Lenor Larsen.

BOTTOM: The house's clean-lined furnishings are supremely compatible with the traditionally spare New England aesthetic.

OPPOSITE PAGE: With its art nouveau glass lamp and 1950s sofa, the living room runs the gamut of twentieth-century style. The cherry chair with walnut inset is by Goodman; the pottery, by Richard Foye.

Shown here, one of the property's extensive gardens.

OPPOSITE PAGE: The potting shed is command central for the farm's elaborate gardens.

CLARKE HOUSE

"I think for a second house you choose a place, not a house," says Puddin Clarke, a Texan for whom the neighboring state of New Mexico is precisely that place. In particular, Santa Fe, with its proximity to nature and its diverse cultural life, was an immediate draw: "You can hike until late in the afternoon, then throw on a sweater and go into town to listen to some chamber music." Besides, her husband, Robert, a lawyer, had grown up in the state.

The couple knew exactly how their house should be. "We wanted to find a traditional pueblo-style adobe," Robert Clarke says. "One that was up high so that we could see the views." His wife came upon just such a place in a piñon forest, overlooking the Sangre de Cristo mountains. If the location was dreamy, the house was not. "It was in unbelievably awful condition," Robert reports. "The plaster had separated from the adobe and there was a three-foot piñon growing outside the kitchen window right in the wall. When the real estate agent brought Puddin to it, she said, 'You don't even want to go in there,' but Puddin said, 'Yes, I do.' Not only did she go inside, she said, 'Bob Clarke is going to love this house.'" The couple hired architect Jake Rodriguez, of Architects Santa Fe, to restore and reconfigure the space.

"When the subcontractors first saw this project they thought we shouldn't bother trying to save it," the architect recalls, but both he and the owners knew it was too good to let go. Rodriguez refurbished the house completely and made some key structural changes. He reoriented the main entrance toward the street and added a new master bedroom, living room, and other areas — doubling the dwelling's size, from twenty-five hundred square feet to five thousand, in the process.

Authenticity was the goal. "We wanted to use mud plaster inside," Robert Clarke says, "and have everything done exactly the way an old adobe ought to be done." In the house's newer portion, Rodriguez used old floor and ceiling materials so that this area would meld seamlessly with the older one. Part of a true adobe's charm lies in the beauty of its beamed ceilings, and even in its new rooms, this house is no exception. There are vigas, or rounded beams, in the master bedroom, square ones in the living room. (The ceiling boards and lintels on the house's two porches, known in these parts as a portal, came from Puddin Clarke's father's Texan ranch.)

As for the house's unique — and very Southwestern — interior, "It's been sort of an evolving situation," Puddin says. She credits a local friend, Maurice Dixon, an authority on New Mexican tin, with help

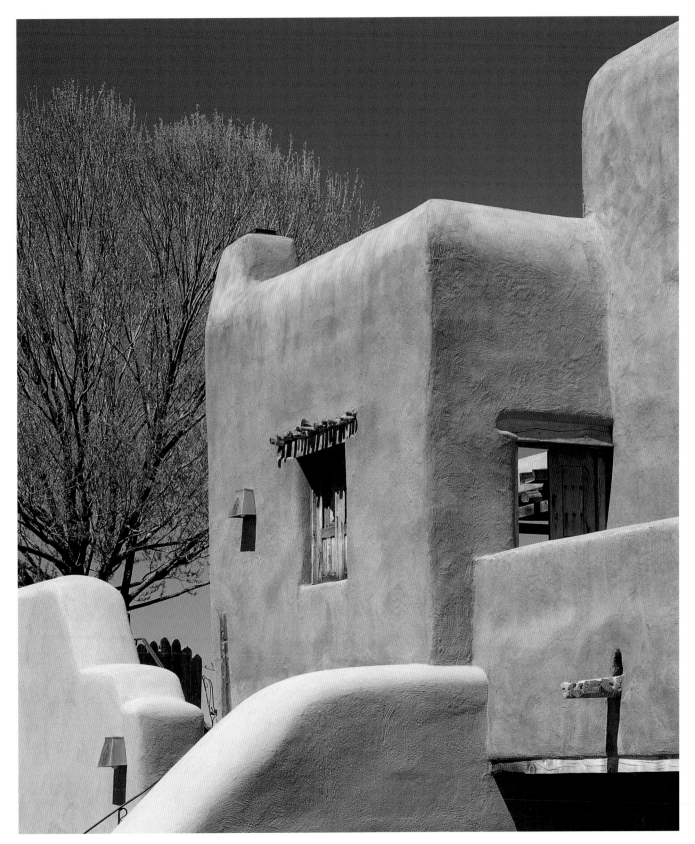

Adobe construction, in which houses are built with layers of dried mud, was originated centuries ago by the Pueblos. This one-story, square-roofed adobe house, which belongs to Puddin and Robert Clarke, is typical of northern New Mexico.

on the "bright, sort of primitive colors" that grace some of the walls, such as yellow in the small library and orange on one of the portals. Another friend, a Houston interior decorator named Ann Eischen, helped with fabrics and furniture placement.

There are plenty of New Mexican pieces here, as well as antiques from both Europe and the New World, including, in the living room, two appealing nineteenth-century painted wood cabinets from Mexico. As for the numerous diverse objects — Native American pots, Hispanic wood carvings, Pueblo miniatures —

displayed throughout, these tend to be local. Robert has a passion for such things. "I have the collector disease," he laughs, and confesses to spending long hours at local art galleries and Santa Fe's famed Indian Market. For her part, Puddin keeps his ever-growing collections artfully arranged ("I'm the fluffer"), adding to them herself from time to time. "If it's nice he bought it, if it's funky, I got it," she teases. Summing up the house, she says, "It's comfortable. It's a place to just relax."

In the master bedroom, a territorial-style fireplace. The mantelpiece was done by Luis Tapia, a Santa Fe wood-carver. The painting is by Victor Goler; the bench is antique New Mexican.

The guest room has a quintessentially New Mexican kiva-style fireplace. The chair and beds, by the famous local artist and furniture maker William Penhallow Henderson, date from the 1930s. The carpets are Navajo.

LEFT: In the newly added living room, an antique New Mexican cross is set on one of a pair of nineteenth-century green Mexican cabinets. The painting above the piano is by Sheldon Parsons, a Santa Fe painter who worked in New Mexico in the early twentieth century. The light fixture is by Maurice Dixon.

BOTTOM RIGHT: On the living room mantelpiece, a study in tin. The candlesticks were made by Maurice Dixon, who did all the house's tinwork; the frame and cross are both early New Mexican.

A still life of Native American pots, artifacts, and local art from the Clarkes' extensive collections.

TOP: In a passageway off the master bedroom, a corner is devoted to crafts. The wood-carvings are by New Mexican artists: the one on the windowsill is by Jay Floyd Lucero; the one of the Virgin Mary, on the table, by Marie Cash. The weaving is an antique Germantown.

BOTTOM: "You can eat in the dining room in your blue jeans," Puddin Clarke says, in praise of the relaxed local style. Contemporary New Mexican pots are displayed in an early American hutch. The painting, by the Santa Fe modernist B. J. O. Nordfeldt, dates from the 1920s or 1930s.

NEAR WATER

~ PINDAR

"Water is best . . ."

This Greek lyric poet also called water "the noblest element," and who would deny it? It refreshes by its very proximity. Even when it's out of sight, it remains tangible. Its presence informs the light, the surrounding vegetation, the air itself. The following six houses aren't coastal homes. You can't delight in the ocean view from their windows, or dive from a dock within view. But the nearby water just may be the reason they exist; vacation houses seem drawn to it, as inevitably as ducks.

The Minnesota property owned by photographer Jim Brandenburg contains dozens of lakes, including an enormous one whose surface he estimates to be thirty-five acres. Even in this woodsy setting, water is a draw. In the winter, we "just ski from one lake to the next to our heart's content," he says. In summer, guests haul canoes into the woods, portaging between pristine bodies of water. Another house in this section — a stately one, not far from the beach in Southampton, New York — is, like so many grand nineteenth-century Hamptons houses, firmly rooted in the land; although you can glimpse a quiet bay from its terrace, it barely acknowledges the presence of the nearby Atlantic. But the very air betrays it, bringing with it a hint of salt and damp, as refreshing as a dip in the ocean.

ELY, MINNESOTA

A FAMILY HOUSE

"It's the loveliest of family houses," says the wife of a New York couple who spend their weekends in a nineteenth-century Hamptons house, a few streets away from the Atlantic Ocean. And she's right. The building in question is a classic, located on an equally classic, tree-lined lane in one of Long Island's most patrician, leafy towns. "It's a real old Southampton house," adds the New York designer Mario Buatta, who did the interior. "It's a good old shingled cottage."

In truth, "cottage" is quite an understatement. The house is vast, with lush, extensive gardens. In Buatta's hands, it has become a place of high color in which the owners' sumptuous collection of orientalia — from ten-foot-tall Indian mandala paintings in the entrance hall to Chinese porcelain vases throughout — is displayed. ("It's a warm-weather house," the husband quips, referring to the collection of Indian art. "I just got some warm-weather art.")

He bought the house in the late 1980s, then turned to Buatta, whom he had known for decades, for help. The designer did substantial renovations, working with a contractor to open up the entrance hall, to square off fussy rooms, and to create a combined library and card room. "We tried to make it as clear as possible," says Buatta, who updated his original interiors a few years ago, after the owner remarried. The couple now share the house with a lively combined family of five children, ranging from toddlers to adults. "It's very much a family house and it's also where we do our entertaining," says the wife.

Known as the "prince of chintz" for his frequent use of that famous printed and glazed cotton cloth, Buatta has been cast against type here, to great effect. The husband initially asked for "no chintz" and, while the designer cheated a bit — there are some lovely draperies of this material in the library, among other places — he mainly complied. What he brought to the equation was glorious color: bright yellow for the entrance hall, red for the library, cool apple green for the drawing room. Through masterful placement of furniture, art, and accessories, he created an environment in which exquisite English antiques, including a massive Georgian desk in the entrance hall, work harmoniously with numerous "Eastern references," as Buatta calls them — and all in a very American house.

Credit for the magnificent flower garden, with its lilac, silver, and gray palette, goes to the wife, who created it from what she calls "just an old garden and one mangy tree." Now, in the English manner, it seems beautifully unrestrained; "I like the wild, untutored look," she says.

"It's quite a dazzler," designer Mario Buatta says of this nineteenth-century Southampton house belonging to a New York couple. The garden, created by the wife, is full of what she describes as "wild and wiry perennials."

"We use it every weekend," she says of the house. "It's nonstop people. Children, friends, drop in all the time. It's just very jolly and open." Much of life here takes place on the porch, which, although perfectly integrated into the original structure, was added by the husband. Here, guests gather for lunch or for drinks before dinner, while children play into the long summer evenings on the surrounding lawn. "We chat and sit out there, surrounded by lots of flowers," the wife says. The family comes here year round; as the temperature drops, they spend more time indoors. From one season to the next, though, one thing remains constant: the hypnotic sound of the nearby sea.

"I wanted the drawing room to be a cool room," Buatta says. "It's an inside room and I wanted it to be cheerful." He had the walls painted in a pale pistachio green. The antique mirror is from Ireland.

RIGHT: In the library, a clutch of family trophies is reflected in the mirror above the mantelpiece. The view through the doorway is of the entrance hall and stairway.

BOTTOM: The newly-created library and card room are painted red for warmth and atmosphere. "The whole thing of the house is just a lot of bright, wonderful colors," the designer says.

TOP: The wife's dressing table, in the master bedroom, features subtle interplay between compatible materials. The blue-and-white linen fabric with a fern motif was originally used, in a chintz version, by decorator Elsie de Wolfe.

BOTTOM: "I kept to a theme of lilacs and silvers and grays with an odd bit of yellow," the wife says of the garden, which she created.

RIGHT: Much weekend activity takes place on the porch, which was added by the owner. Buatta describes its artfully arranged furnishings as "a hodgepodge of things." The lake beyond is a favorite gathering spot for geese.

SHAPIRO LOG CABIN

Almost invariably, the true weekend house involves a certain relaxation of taste. Certainly that's the case for Berta Shapiro, a Chicago-based interior designer who spends most of her time in a relatively formal city apartment containing some truly perfect antiques. Come Friday afternoon, though, she's apt to round up friends and family and head east, driving along the southern shore of Lake Michigan to a charming cabin in the woods, a stone's throw from the Great Lake itself.

In its own quiet way, southwestern Michigan is a center for fine design; such noted Chicago architects as Stanley Tigerman, Margaret McCurry, and Lawrence Booth, among others, have all built houses in the region. Shapiro's place, which was originally a mail-order cabin assembled from a kit, may have more prosaic origins, but in her hands it has become a place of quintessential weekend style, witty and low-keyed.

She bought the cabin from an earlier owner years ago; subsequently, with the help of architect John Morris of Morris Architects and Planners in Chicago, she revamped it, adding a dining room, fireplace, and screened-in porch — a necessity for Michigan summers. ("We spend a lot of time on the porch," she says. "It's just a dream. Screened porches are essential.") Morris also transformed the existing staircase and added French windows. "It was a house of very few windows and only one or two doors," Shapiro recalls. "Now it's open everywhere to the outside."

Inside, it's a triumph of casual style. "It's really just comfortable furniture and objects that I like," the designer says. There is a carpenter's level tacked to the wall ("It looked like a nice bit of decorative molding"); a birdhouse collection in a converted garage, which is now used as a second living room or studio; and, in the main room, distressed blue shelving that once did service in a general store. With its antique English candlewick bedspreads and numerous other vintage materials, the cabin also reflects its owner's love of beautiful textiles and handicrafts.

Like every self-respecting artist, Shapiro isn't above purloining things she admires. She calls the delightful white dining room a "rip-off from Carl Larsson," the nineteenth-century Swedish illustrator and designer. She came upon a picture of Larsson's own dining room in a book on Scandinavian style, loved it, and made it her own: with its white walls, pale green trim, and potted ivy trained around its windows, the room is almost an exact duplicate of Larsson's. The extended windowsill, which wraps around the room, is enlivened by the addition of an ever-shifting gallery of "things I love," Shapiro says, including beach glass from the shore of nearby Lake Michigan and a postcard by the Romantic painter Caspar David Friedrich.

The house's very weekendness — the fact that Shapiro spends relatively short periods of time there — can bring with it certain frustrations. She hints wistfully at the things she would do if she had more time. "I'd just putter more and paint little moldings." Even so, her house is a perfect — and perfectly cozy — place to decompress, just as it is. And that, after all, is what the best weekends are about.

Interior designer Berta Shapiro's cabin was made from a kit by the previous owners. Later, she added to it. In contrast to this rustic facade, the cabin's interior is full of pretty, light touches, from baskets full of pinecones to antique fabrics draped over the backs of sofas and chairs.

"I just love the various forms," Shapiro says of the birdhouse collection in her studio. Other shelves reveal her love of humble, yet beautiful, objects, including vintage hardware and ceramics.

OPPOSITE PAGE: "This was meant as a studio and gardening room, but it really became another living room," the owner says of the converted garage. She added French doors and lots of interesting furniture and textiles. The cobalt blue gateleg table is mid-nineteenth-century Swedish.

TOP RIGHT: Within close walking distance of Lake Michigan, Shapiro's house is in constant weekend use, with a steady stream of visitors, including family and friends.

BOTTOM LEFT: "This is where we come first thing in the morning," Shapiro says of her screened porch. It contains an assortment of casual furniture, from an Adirondack sofa to a folding French park chair.

OPPOSITE PAGE: In the master bedroom, some classic Americana. The black-painted center table is from the late 1800s; the blue chest of drawers and rag rug are both from the early twentieth century.

Shapiro took the idea for her dining room, which was added to the house, from the cottage of Carl Larsson, the Swedish illustrator. The antique American corner cupboard was raised to fit the space.

THREE PARTNERS' FISHING CABIN

BITTERROOT VALLEY, MONTANA

"It was love at first sight," Larry Mindel reports. "I fell in love with the Bitterroot Valley, the trout, the fishing, the birds, and everything else." Invited to visit this corner of Montana by a friend who owns land on the Bitterroot River, Mindel found himself reluctant to leave. So much so that he and a couple of friends (who, like himself, are "passionate, passionate fly fishermen," he says) came up with an idea: why not build a cabin here, share it, and fish as much as they like?

As to who would design the place, Mindel had no doubt. As the founder of Il Fornaio, the well-known group of Italian-inspired restaurants and bakeries, he had worked easily for years with architect Howard Backen, who has offices in both San Francisco and Marin County. Since Backen has designed numerous log cabin–like structures — a style that's almost a requirement if you build in this state — he was clearly the man for the job. The fact that his wife, Lori O'Kane Backen (of Lori O'Kane Design), is an interior designer whose "hobby is Adirondack furniture," as Mindel puts it, only made the choice more perfect.

"They wanted a place where they could play poker in the back room and clean their fish on the docks," O'Kane Backen recalls. "They wanted it rustic, cozy, and warm." Howard Backen isn't exaggerating when he says that he and his designing wife had a free hand on this project — in fact, the cabin's partners, all businessmen based in Northern California, were all so busy that none of them even saw the place until it was done.

Because many different groups would be using the house — all of them, presumably, wanting to socialize — Backen designed it to be as open as possible, with a kitchen that overlooks the dining and living areas. He put in lots of sleeping spaces, including two master bedrooms and a classic, twelve-foot-deep screened-in porch that overlooks the Bitterroot Mountains ("People fight over who gets to sleep out there," according to Mindel). With the cabin's sleeping lofts, bunk rooms, and other spaces, "you could sleep twelve with no problem," he adds.

You could say that Montana itself dictated the interior design, which is inescapably Western. O'Kane Backen filled the house with third-phase Navajo rugs ("they're very simple, clean lined, beautiful," she says), using them as "a kind of platform on which to build." As for the rest, she and her husband designed some witty, Western-inspired furniture, including a built-in sofa with a scene in marquetry of a bear drinking from a jug. An extraordinary antler-and-sheepskin chandelier, by Peter Sillerup for the Utah company Wild West

This classic Western fishing cabin, by architect Howard Backen, is located on Montana's Bitterroot River, in the southern tip of the valley of the same name.

73

Late afternoon on the screened porch. The porch wraps around three sides of the house. The view is of a sweep of lawn heading down to the Bitterroot River, which is lined with cottonwood trees.

Designs, illuminates the long sugar-pine dining table. As for the stuffed grizzly who calmly surveys the entrance hall, he just appeared one day, thanks to one of the partners. Mindel says, "I got there and there it was."

The three owners draw a lottery to determine their schedules. "We share common wine and common everything and it's never been a hassle," Mindel says. He typically spends a total of a month here each year in a large group that includes his wife, Debby, a school-teacher; five children, and four grandchildren. "We're like our own band of vagabonds," he observes. The family rides regularly at a

"world-class equestrian center" in the neighborhood; a newly built local golf course has introduced them to a whole other sport. Most of all, Mindel says, "We enjoy the beauty of Montana."

As for Backen, he and his wife are friends of the Mindels; when they visit the cabin, they have the rare experience of being able to enjoy, on a regular basis, an environment they created for someone else. They spend their nights there on the sleeping porch, where — appearances to the contrary — it's often anything but quiet. "The lightning storms out there are phenomenal," Backen reports. "It just couldn't be better."

TOP: As they do in nature, this bear in the hall just turned up, an unexpected gift from one of the cabin's partners. The side table was inspired by Thomas Molesworth. The Navajo rugs were actually woven in Mexico.

BOTTOM LEFT: The three partners who share this fishing lodge "wanted it to be cozy," interior designer Lori O'Kane Backen says. In the living room are leather armchairs from National Upholstery, a Molesworth-inspired built-in sofa, and a Navajo carpet.

BOTTOM RIGHT: In the dining room are a fanciful antler chandelier by artist Peter Sillerup for Wild West Designs and chairs by Old Hickory. The pine cupboard is an American antique.

In a guest room are twin beds with a cowboy motif, designed by Lori O'Kane Backen. "Her touches inside were marvelous," co-owner Larry Mindel says.

OPPOSITE PAGE: The twelve-foot-deep screened porch of this Montana fishing cabin is "a classic," architect Howard Backen says. With its view of the Bitterroot Mountains, it's a much-sought-after place to spend the night.

BANKER HOUSE

WATER MILL, NEW YORK

When Pamela Banker, a New York interior designer, moved into what she describes as a "little cottage with a small garden" in the town of Water Mill, in the Hamptons, it really was a kind of coming home. She'd spent childhood weekends and summers in her family's enormous Stanford White–designed house in nearby Southampton; later, she and her husband, David, a financial advisor, lived part-time in another building on that property.

But then their lives took a non-Hamptons turn. For fifteen years they weekended in a large house on Long Island's North Shore, about two hours away. But that place turned out to be "much too big for the way it was used, about twenty-five weekends a year," Banker says, and several years ago the couple returned to the South Shore in search of a smaller place. "My roots here made coming back very desirable," she says. "We love being back here. The light and the air are terrific."

The structure they found, a shingle house that measures about thirty-five hundred square feet and has four bedrooms, is simplicity itself. So was the process of decorating it, according to Banker, who recently returned to her own practice — Pamela Banker Associates — after spending five years with the New York decorating firm of Parish-Hadley Associates (a period that ended when Albert Hadley, that company's legendary partner, retired and closed the firm).

From the outside, the residence, which overlooks Mecox Bay, looks as traditional as they come. But, in fact, it was built in 1970. In keeping with its style — and her own — Banker opted for a pretty, easy-going interior. "This house is cozy country," she says. "It's full of things like baskets and pine furniture, even a cherry highboy. It's a very relaxing place. It's not overly decorated — just a cozy place to put our feet up."

The interior came easily. Both Bankers had inherited antiques from their families, so there was nothing to buy. "It was as though this house was meant to happen, just the way everything fit in," Pamela says. And the structure's relative newness meant that, apart from painting a few rooms and placing seagrass floor coverings on some unloved floors, there was blessedly little to be done. Some of the more striking touches, such as the living room paneling done in Williamsburg blue, were already in place. Banker's main task — besides some artful furniture placement — was to improve what

"It's very simple and livable," interior designer Pamela Banker says of her Long Island house. The curtain and upholstery fabric, by Brunschwig & Fils, has figured in earlier Banker houses. "This is the fourth life it's had," she says.

With its myriad tennis rackets, golf clubs, and gardening clogs, the entrance hall reveals exactly how weekends are spent at this Hamptons home.

OPPOSITE PAGE: In the southwest corner of the living room, Brunschwig & Fils fabric echoes the pale tones of a Turkish kilim. The prints are of quadrupeds — not birds! — by John James Audubon, the nineteenth-century ornithologist and artist.

was already present, such as by painting part of the living room wall white, for a two-toned effect.

By happenstance, the blue in the multicolored fabric by Brunschwig & Fils used for both the window treatment and slipcovers matched the walls perfectly, only adding to the designer's feeling that this house was meant to be. "I brought that fabric into my life about eighteen years ago," she recalls, adding that it has now figured into its fourth weekend residence.

For the Bankers, country life is a succession of low-keyed days. "I just love to collapse and get away from the world when I'm here. I love to ride my bike and putter in the garden," Pamela says. Her husband spends his time catching up on his tennis, and both love riding their bikes to the nearby organic fruit and vegetable stand to pick up fresh produce for the evening meal. "It's a very serene situation," the decorator says of her Hamptons life. "Just a very rustic feeling."

TOP LEFT: On a living room table are a trove of American objects from the nineteenth century, including a blue glass pitcher, a lamp made of glazed pottery, and papier-mâché dishes.

BOTTOM RIGHT: The dining room is reflected in a black-and-gilt painted mirror. The wood-and-wicker basket is nineteenth-century American. The crewel-work curtains belonged to Pam Banker's grandmother.

OPPOSITE PAGE: In a pretty corner of the study, garden colors predominate. The polished red chintz fabric is from Brunschwig & Fils; the window and sofa fabric is from Alan Campbell; the hand-painted pillow is by Christina Horn. The rug is antique Oushak.

RAVENWOOD

Talk about getting away from it all. When nature photographer Jim Brandenburg travels from his home near Minneapolis to Ravenwood, his compound near the Canadian border, he enters one of the largest wilderness regions in America — one and a half million square miles of pure, unadulterated nature. Not only are there no roads in this federally owned and protected area, known as the Boundary Waters Canoe Area Wilderness, but no planes are allowed to fly overhead. Which is exactly how Brandenburg, who made his name shooting for *National Geographic* magazine and is known for his studies of wolves, likes it.

He first bought land here about twenty-five years ago, at which time he had a cabin, guest house, and sauna built. Then, about a decade ago, he vowed to spend more time in the woods. Brandenburg had come to a point where "I mentally and creatively had reached the limit," he says. "I'd sort of burned out." Although he had "seen the most exotic places in the world," what he needed was a dose of rural Minnesota. In a five-year project, he and architect David Salmela transformed part of his fifteen-hundred acres into a kind of working compound, one that has the feel of an ancient Viking village.

"My task was to expand this place into a studio and home," Salmela says. "My goal was not to upstage the log structures in any way, and to use them as a nucleus for the expansion." As is common in this region, there were Scandinavian overtones: the original cabin had been built to resemble a *stabur*, a kind of storage facility that is ubiquitous in the Norwegian countryside, with a larger second story cantilevered out over the first.

For the new buildings, Salmela, who is of Finnish extraction, and Brandenburg, whose roots are in Norway, also wanted to pay homage to the area's "vernacular ties," as the architect puts it. He created a cascading-roofed studio, one that connects with the original one by way of a versatile, low-ceilinged transitional area that acts as a gallery, dining area, and entry space. He also added a guest studio and sod-roofed garage, partially built into a hillside. And he positioned new and old buildings so that "they're very quaint and very close, the way the houses were arranged by the first settlers." In a nod to his ancestors' building habits, Salmela kept the scale small (the studio building measures only fifteen feet wide, the guest studio a mere ten feet) and used rich natural materials. For the roofs alone, he used, variously, sod, shake, lapboard, and other elements. Because the buildings' exterior walls are stained black, they seem to settle into the landscape.

Brandenburg and his wife, Judy, who runs the studio, kept the compound's interiors simple, letting its exceptional level of craftsmanship speak for itself. Many of the furnishings come from other parts of the world, from the French modernist chrome-and-wicker rocking chair acquired a quarter of a century ago to the fanciful Swedish lamps, made of paper-thin cedar, that illuminate both dining table and fireplace.

Architect David Salmela juxtaposed new structures with older ones in this northern Minnesota compound, positioning them close together in the manner of the ancient Vikings.

TOP: This imposing moose skull dominates the porch of the guest cabin, an older building that Brandenburg describes as "a hopelessly romantic little log thing."

BOTTOM LEFT: Ravenwood abuts the Boundary Waters Canoe Area Wilderness, which contains more than a thousand lakes. "You could paddle your canoe from one of these lakes to another for the rest of your life and never see the same one twice," according to Brandenburg.

BOTTOM RIGHT: "The waterfall is the focal point," says Brandenburg. He copied the design for the sod-roofed sauna house (one of Ravenwood's original buildings) from a Finnish magazine. The swinging chair was custom made.

"I'm one of those crazy people who can't separate life from work," Brandenburg cheerfully admits. At Ravenwood, he doesn't need to. He calls the place his "picture farm" and it's decidedly a working retreat, a perfect spot from which to observe and photograph moose and other wildlife. Everything here revolves around his art: the transitional space between the buildings, which Brandenburg describes as "long and narrow like a little theater," is used for seminars and slide shows; the sod-roofed camera room, with its mutton windows, is used for equipment storage. Even the couple's guests, who tend to be outdoor writers, editors, friends, and family, often turn up with work in mind.

As for that burnout, it's gone. "This house and this whole experience really gave me a transfusion of hope and excitement," he explains. Things, in fact, have come full circle: Ravenwood brought Brandenburg back to his work, while he, in turn, has transformed it into art. One of his latest books — *Chased by the Light*, published by Northword — celebrates the wildlife to be found in his own neck of the woods.

"There's an ongoing mystery to it," architect Salmela says of Ravenwood. Among its most enigmatic sights: a two-hundred-pound rock suspended from a cable, designed by owner Jim Brandenburg as a moving sculpture. Behind it is a folkloric-looking guest structure.

In the "brook-viewing room," a modernist tableau. The cherry-doweled interior wall was inspired by a story on bamboo that Brandenburg photographed for *National Geographic*. The Japanese-style bench, of Douglas fir, is of his own design. The photograph on the wall is Brandenburg's *Dream Back the Bison* (1991).

TOP LEFT: The dining niche, as seen from the entryway. The lacquered bowl, by Donna Karan, is filled with Japanese river rocks. The cherry table, cabinets, and shelves were designed by Brandenburg and Salmela and built by brothers Brad and Curt Holmes.

TOP RIGHT: From a specially designed window in this three-story studio space, Brandenburg photographs passing wildlife. The unfinished raw cedar paneling is by Brad and Curt Holmes. The metal-and-mesh chair is an "Aeron" by Bill Stumpf for Herman Miller.

BOTTOM: Tony, one of the family's two Italian greyhounds, surveys the living room. Sofas are Danish, by M. Eilersen. The steel table is by Room & Board, a Minnesota company.

A COUPLE'S HOUSE

WATER MILL, NEW YORK

Sometimes a country house flagrantly defies our notion of what weekending is all about. One such place belongs to a couple in Water Mill, New York, a town the owner describes as "sort of in Southampton." For this Manhattanite and her husband, whose children are grown, their time out here has nothing to do with dressing in torn jeans and weathered boat shoes, or going to clambakes on the beach, or having friends camp out on the lawn. As delightful as such experiences may be, they're simply irrelevant here. Instead, a certain formality prevails. "It doesn't look like a beach house," the owner says of her house. "It has more of a city feeling."

She and her husband had admired a house by Mark Zeff (described by its creator as "very relaxed, colonial, and clean-feeling"), so they turned to this New York–based architect and interior designer for their weekend home. They didn't want a grand house — "just a pied-à-terre in the country," the owner says. Their property was also fairly small and this fact, as much as anything, dictated its final style. "The scale of the house called for a mixture of farmhouse and colonial South African and English manor house," Zeff says. "It's a hybrid English cottage."

When you're within these walls you have the delicious feeling of being somewhere else. Somewhere exotic, that is: in India under the Raj; on a Central American plantation; in a Paris 1920s-era *hôtel particulier*. "It's sort of breathtaking when you come in the front door," the owner reports. "With its square columns at the entrance, it's different from every other house in the Hamptons. It's sort of a traditional house. On the other hand it's very Eastern." The living room, in particular, with its crisp white walls and tawny-shaded furniture, has a colonial edge. Throughout the house, intricately carved wooden detailing heightens this feeling. "I wanted it to have a handmade sensibility," the architect says.

Because Zeff designed the interiors, architecture, and much of the furniture, the house has an unusually consistent style. "There's a lot of relationship from one room to another," as he puts it, "a lot of connection." The stairway's intriguingly curved, African-inspired newel posts, for example, are echoed in the posts of the master bedroom's four-poster bed. And Zeff repeated a curved rope pattern from the house's two eighteenth-century wooden mantelpieces (found at Manhattan's famed Sixth Avenue flea market) in the study's wall paneling and built-in shelves. Many of the pieces here, including a Biedermeier game table in the charming reading alcove at the top of the stairs, are antiques; even so, they fit right in.

If this sixty-one-hundred-square-foot residence seems all of a piece, that's just as it should be, its owner believes. "We don't like things that aren't a hundred percent," she says. The couple's weekend place may not be casual, but the time they spend in and around it generally is. Typically, they pass warmer days outdoors, playing tennis and golf or just enjoying the beach. In the evening they like having small groups of people for dinner. The way the house evolved still strikes the owner as miraculous. "We wanted a little shack, but look what we have — a *very* nice shack."

Like numerous elements in this house in Water Mill, New York, a caned teak chair from Indonesia recalls Anglo-Indian, or colonial, style.
Beyond the window are a pool and a structure that architect Mark Zeff describes as a "very cottagey" cabana.

TOP: The bookworm's perfect weekend. . . . The sofa in this upstairs reading nook was built for the space; the game table is Swedish Biedermeier. On the walls are nineteenth-century English golfing prints.

BOTTOM LEFT: "What I like about this house is the flow of rooms," the owner says. Placed in one intriguing corner, in front of a second-floor bedroom, are an English secretary and chair, both nineteenth century.

BOTTOM RIGHT: "It's breathtaking when you come in," the owner says of her Long Island house. This view from the entrance hall to the living room reveals its Anglo-Indian sensibility and palette. The leather lamp is by Mark Zeff; the art deco bronzes are from the owners' collection.

OPPOSITE PAGE: In the master bedroom, the bedposts' distinctive swirly shape is repeated in the bedside lamp (both designed by Zeff) and, indeed, throughout the house. The black painted bedside tables are also by Zeff.

AMONG VINEYARDS

~ THE BIBLE (CORINTHIANS:9:7)

"Who planteth a vineyard?"

Wine has its obvious enticements, but who has ever stopped to consider the addictive quality of vineyards? Every house in this section speaks of them, in one way or another. The following dwellings are located in Napa and Sonoma counties, which together form the preeminent wine-growing region of the United States. Oenophilia has brought a sophistication to these contiguous counties, with those who build here often taking their design cues from the venerable wine-growing regions of Italy and France.

Exceptional people come to live here, sometimes for exceptional reasons, such as the man who commissioned architect Ricardo Legorreta's Casa Cabernet (shown on pages 96 – 103). He one day woke up to the conviction that he had to have a vineyard. "It was so odd for a Midwesterner, I thought the idea would go away," his wife recalls. It didn't, and there was nothing for it but to head out to Napa to shop for land.

Three of the following residences — including Casa Cabernet, the Thornton family's rammed earth house, and an evocative stone residence in a former distillery — are owned by part-time wine growers. The owners of the other two have little to do, directly, with wine. Even so, like everyone in this viticultural region, they have come to feel a part of its annual agricultural rhythms, from planting to first crush. This ancient cycle draws us to it, much like vineyards themselves.

HEALDSBURG, CALIFORNIA.

CASA CABERNET

NAPA VALLEY, CALIFORNIA

"He's constantly bringing you face to face with the earth," a client says of the Mexican architect Ricardo Legorreta, who designed a country house for her and her husband in California's Napa Valley. This brightly colored, organic-looking residence sits on top of a mountain on the couple's ninety acres, about thirty of them vineyards. Looking out through the house's slatted windows, "you're brought face to face with the pinecones, bark, twigs, and fallen leaves," in the owner's words.

As conceived by both Legorreta and his son, Victor (both of Legorreta Arquitectos, Mexico City), the house is full of the elements — experiences, really — we've come to expect from this team: an enigmatic entrance courtyard where enormous boulders divert attention from the door; an infinity-edged pool that laps against the living room's exterior wall; an outdoor stairway that looks as if it leads precisely nowhere. (The local architect on the project was Brooks Walker III of Walker/Warner Architects, San Francisco.)

The owners, a couple who live in the Midwest but spend long weekends and holidays in Napa, wanted a sense of intimacy and a close relationship with the land. "The solution was to break out the different elements of the house into four main volumes," Legorreta says. The architect came up with a multipavilioned house, with one structure containing a living room and kitchen and another the master bedroom and bath. Guest rooms, which can be entered separately, are housed in two other areas. "This solution permitted us to create different environments in each one," Legorreta says. "It also let us take advantage of the different vistas of the property."

The master bedroom and living room are joined by a long galleria, a very Legorretian transitional space that suggests contemplation, meditation, and privacy. The main pavilions, which overlook a terrace made of tikul, or Mexican limestone, and a cobalt blue lap pool, are oriented around water; the guest structures are more rooted in the woods. As conceived by Legorreta and local landscape architect Jack Chandler, "the landscaping is basically trying to restore the site to the natural woods that it was, trying to make it look like we never disturbed it at all," the owner says. "Every piece of stone came from this site. It was really a harmonious coming together of the materials."

"The kind of trees, the color of the earth, called for the darker color," architect Richard Legorreta says of this Napa Valley house's facade. The close integration of water into the design is one of this architect's hallmarks.

Architect Ricardo Legorreta loves mystery, and this outdoor staircase, in stained cast concrete, has more than its share. It leads from the main pavilion of the Napa Valley home to the guest pavilions.

The view from the courtyard. Beyond the madrones, wild oaks, and other native trees lies the lap pool and an incomparable view of the Napa Valley.

As for color of the exterior walls, she recalls Legorreta exclaiming "Earth and blood!" as the painted model of the house was unveiled. "The next day, we said, 'That color isn't earth and blood, it's cabernet.' The next plans came in with the name Casa Cabernet, and it stuck." So did the color, which reminded the couple of the red bark of madrone trees and felt right from the outset.

Architecture was only part of the project; most of the furniture was custom made by the architects. "I don't believe in marking a line between architecture and interior," Legorreta says. "To me, the interior is the important space." There is an inspired consistency to the finished design, with recurring elements, including a ubiquitous grid pattern, uniting the interior and exterior spaces. Color, too, pulls disparate rooms and elements together.

"Ricardo really designed everything," the wife says, pointing out a clean-lined desk of old Mexican wood in the master bedroom and, in the dining alcove off the living room, a rough-hewn, almost folkloric dinner table, made to the exact width of the window behind it. Other pieces were the result of a spirited collaboration between both parties. One of these, a Louisiana cypress bed enclosure in the master bedroom, threatened never to be done. "Time was moving on," the husband recalls. "Ricardo came up one day with a little model, like a dollhouse version. We said we liked it. I said, 'Is that to scale? We don't have time for drawings. Why don't we just take it over to the woodworker.' So we did." From the architect's point of view, such fluid, collaborative design moments are a sure sign of success: "If my clients have the feeling that they designed the house together with me — that's when I've done a good job."

The living pavilion seen almost in its entirety. The red freestanding wall separates the kitchen from the living and dining areas. The house's entrance is to the right.

"It feels to me like a cloister walk," the wife says of the mysterious galleria that connects the living area with the bedroom pavilion.

TOP RIGHT: "One of Ricardo's principles is the framed view," the wife says. From the dining table, the view in question is of the cobalt blue lap pool. The table and chairs were custom made by Legorreta Arquitectos.

BOTTOM LEFT: Throughout the house, color and patterns recur. Here, the deep red of the facade is echoed at the window grille, as is a ubiquitous grid pattern that can be found, in one form or another, in almost every room.

OPPOSITE PAGE: In the living room, the very Legorretian elements of color, light, and water. All furniture not designed by Legorreta Arquitectos was approved by them for the house. Chairs are by Wicker Wicker Wicker; fabric is by Ralph Lauren.

HILL/GILLIAM RESIDENCE

GLEN ELLEN, CALIFORNIA

Located on more than thirty woodsy acres in Glen Ellen, California, the Italianate house Fred Hill and Peter Gilliam share is a bright focal point in its dense green surroundings. Its yellow walls and periwinkle shutters are as brightly colored as the hydrangeas and Spanish geraniums that, in season, grow in the walled courtyard before it. It took about thirty samples to get the color of the exterior walls exactly right, according to Gilliam, who is an interior designer.

The two men bought this Sonoma County land more than a decade ago, drilled a well, and bought an extraordinary set of rustic eighteenth-century doors they'd found in London to grace their future weekend retreat. They didn't rush to build. Instead, they went back to their busy lives in San Francisco, where Gilliam works with John Wheatman & Associates and Fred is one of the West Coast's preeminent literary agents, with offices both there and in Los Angeles.

Shrewdly, Hill and Gilliam rented a cottage for a couple of years in the nearby Napa Valley to get a sense of what weekending in California's wine country is all about. They soon realized that life there is conducted, as much as possible, outdoors. For their house's design, they looked to Italy. "Their vision was a cross between a Palladian villa and a Tuscan farmhouse," remarks John Field of the San Francisco firm of Field Paoli Architects, who transformed the two men's ideas into viable architectural plans.

Together, they oriented the house in a way that does justice to its rich surroundings. Everywhere, it opens up to nature. Beyond the broad terrace and infinity pool, the house overlooks a rich, vineyard-lined valley; in other directions it affords a woodland view of manzanitas, scrub oaks, and other Californian trees. "The idea was really to do an open-air pavilion," says Gilliam, who points out that there are only two actual windows in the house; the rest are French doors. The alternating oval and square clerestory windows were inspired by a book on Venetian palazzos.

The house, with its symmetric wings, is entered via an ample breezeway. To the left, through the imposing Mediterranean-style doors, lies the living room, kitchen, and master bedroom suite; to the right is a guest suite that could tempt any visitor to overstay. Offices for both Hill and Gilliam, in the same wing, double as guest rooms.

"Fred is the great gardener," Peter Gilliam says of partner Fred Hill. On the pergola are blue wisteria and two kinds of roses, icebergs and banksiae.

Gilliam calls the house an "oasis"; he and Hill clearly delight in the private, restorative weekends they spend within, and around, its walls. Time here is about the important things: gardening — mainly potted plants, including bougainvillea and Amber Queen roses, among other varieties — reading, movie watching, and visits from friends.

The interior, which was designed by Gilliam, bears witness to its owners' love of travel — recent trips have taken them to Egypt and South America — and of beautiful things. Almost everything was bought specifically for the house. "We'd both fall in love with something and just make it work in the space," Gilliam recalls. Jean-Michel Frank chairs, an outsize Aalto vase, and other vestiges of

modernism are combined with some much-loved antiques, including the living room's French tavern table, which dates from the seventeenth century. The Directoire bed in Hill's study, from a favorite shop in Avignon, seemed incomplete until he came across the Patagonian fox blanket of his dreams, complete with tails ("It's so politically incorrect," he enthuses), on a recent trip to Argentina.

Given the house's addictive tranquility and the fact that each man can conduct many aspects of his career from his country office, it's no wonder that Hill and Gilliam's weekends are becoming almost shamefully extended. "By now we're here four or five nights a week," Gilliam says, looking a bit sheepish at the confession. But only a bit.

TOP LEFT: What every well-appointed study needs . . . In Hill's office, a library ladder with cantilevered bookshelves; a Directoire bed with urns; a fur throw from Patagonia. The photograph (of busts in the Boston Athenaeum) is by Marie Coscindas.

BOTTOM RIGHT: In a corner of the living room, an antique Chinese red lacquer chest faces off against a Louis XVI console. Gilliam bought the washbowl above the chest in Barcelona. The handblown vase is by Alvar Aalto.

OPPOSITE PAGE: "The furniture plan is pretty strict," says owner Gilliam, who did the house's interior design. In the living room, a Jean-Michel Frank–inspired sofa is upholstered in Italian chartreuse velvet. The lamp is by Italian architect Gae Aulenti.

LEFT: A view from the guest wing of the Hill/Gilliam house, through the entrance breezeway, to the main wing. The rafters, like the house's shutters, are painted a distinctive periwinkle.

RIGHT: A view of the doors that started it all. Bought in London, they partly inspired the house. The painting is *Burrito* (1993), by John Register. The octagonal table in brushed stainless steel was designed by Peter Gilliam.

OPPOSITE PAGE: At home in Sonoma County, "the biggest luxury we have is privacy," Gilliam says. Here, a table for two in the walled courtyard at the front of the house.

A WOMAN'S HOUSE

In California's Napa Valley, wine is in the air. Vineyards stretch out in every direction. Locals chat about vintages and varietals as easily as the weather, and people who have never considered a life in wine seem to do so, routinely, after driving down vineyard-lined roads, stopping off to try a perfect pinot at one winery, a deep-toned zinfandel at another.

As more and more people are discovering, a wine-centered life can be had on a part-time basis. At least that's true for a San Franciscan who spends her weekends, often with her grown-up children, on three hundred and fifty acres in Napa, almost ninety of which are vineyards. Besides delighting in the countryside itself, with its relatively balmy climate, the family takes part in the prevailing culture, bringing their grape harvest each year to a local winery where it is transformed into merlot and cabernet.

For her weekend retreat, the owner asked Marc LaRoche, an architect with offices in San Francisco and on Bainbridge Island, Washington, to restore an old distillery on her land. "I said, 'Let's gut it and come up with some great ideas,'" she recalls. Built in 1904, the distillery was as solid and dank as its former function implies.

"It's hard to conceive of how dark these rooms were," LaRoche says. It subsequently became a state senator's summer home and, later, a bed-and-breakfast establishment. In both incarnations, it acquired some embellishments. The politician added "a bit of a medieval theme," the architect says. "There was a circular turret on the exterior patio and a heavy, dark oak-paneled library inside." In its time as a B & B, other changes, including "a lot of slapdash plaster work" took place, he adds. "It was all pretty tacky."

Opening up this gloomy structure was a priority for LaRoche — "Natural light is a big part of what I do," he asserts — and he eventually added expansive windows. But first he gutted the interior and did a seismic retrofit, a necessity in earthquake-prone California. He wanted to create a crisply modern house that paid homage to its

In good weather, much of weekend life at this Napa Valley house takes place on one of two dining terraces off the kitchen. This one affords a glorious view of the garden.

Because of scheduling constraints, the architect replaced the original pool and pool house, adding terraces, before tackling the main house.

own "primitive early construction," he says, and much of the strength of the final design comes from the way it consistently juxtaposes old and new. "I tried to impart a new sense of contemporary detailing that would contrast with this very heavy, very rustic old building."

The result is a perfect distillation. The owner loves wood and stone; LaRoche worked his magic on both elements, brightening the once-grim stone and adding lots of clean wooden detailing. Every room seems to contain something surprising. A basket-weave ceiling graces the living room; in the library, some Scandinavian-looking bookshelves are scaled via a sleek, rolling steel ladder. As arresting as such touches might be, LaRoche took pains not to overdo them: "I try not to load up spaces with too many tricks, but select one that will have the best impact."

For the interiors, "the goal was to strike a balance between the rough-hewn nature of the existing building with the refinement of select furniture of our times," says Trina LaRoche of Carter LaRoche Interior Design. The designer, who is the architect's wife, added contemporary furnishings, from the natural-shaded carpet in the living room by Allegra Hicks for Christopher Farr to some sharp, and sharp-edged, furniture by Ted Boerner in the master bedroom.

Happily, from the designer's point of view, the client had "a keen interest in contemporary design and welcomed the avant-garde." So, for that matter, does this retreat. Architect, designer, and client all shared an unusually compatible vision — and it shows, both inside and out. Thanks to their alchemy, the ancient culture of wine has become both daring and new.

TOP: "It's just an incredible site," says architect Marc LaRoche. This view of the Napa Valley with its acres of vineyards and rolling hills, taken from one of the house's terraces, proves his point.

BOTTOM LEFT: The kitchen mixes country furniture with cutting-edge style. The owner chose the cabinets' pale green color to match designer Trina LaRoche's eye color. Appliances include a Thermador stove; beaded hanging lamps are by Flos.

BOTTOM RIGHT: In the dining room are a Harvest table and console by Ted Burner. The woven back of the maple nest chairs by Montina matches the basket-weave ceiling in the living room.

113

TOP RIGHT: In a house that seems fascinated by stone and wood, the staircase makes use of both. Architect LaRoche interwove maple slats with sandblasted stainless steel rods for a modern, yet timeless, effect.

BOTTOM LEFT: "Some people are averse to punching openings into a big old stone building, but I'm not," says Marc LaRoche. Large windows and a vaulted ceiling of hemlock-veneered interlaced plywood brighten the living room. The "gilda" lounge chair is by Zanotta.

LEFT: In the library, a stainless steel library ladder designed by Marc LaRoche matches the sandblasted backs of square "Oscar" chairs by Inno. (Their seats are woven leather.) The couch is "HighNoon" from Ladel.

RIGHT: In the bathroom, as elsewhere, the LaRoches juxtaposed modern design with older elements for a mutually beneficial effect. With its archetypal shape, the Philippe Starck–designed bathtub fits right in.

TOP AND OPPOSITE PAGE: In the master bedroom of this Napa Valley residence, crisp modern furnishings work beautifully with the house's stone walls. The bed and night table are by Ted Boerner; the lamp is from Donghia. The draperies, designed by interior designer Trina LaRoche, are made from four kinds of silk.

BOTTOM: Sundown over the Napa Valley.

WEISMAN/FISHER POOL PAVILION

HEALDSBURG, CALIFORNIA

Ask Jeffry Weisman how many bedrooms his weekend pool pavilion contains and he'll answer, exuberantly, "None!" Which is exactly the point. Although the structure he describes as "a classic French pavilion with doors on all sides and high windows" has an airy elegance, it's decidedly not grandiose. In fact, it is a one-room residence, measuring seventeen by thirty-four feet.

When Weisman and his partner, Andrew Fisher, both interior designers, first built the pavilion on their twenty-seven acres in Sonoma County's Russian River Valley, they considered it a temporary dwelling. "We thought, why not build the pool house first, then build the pool and see how we use it?" he recalls. "Then we'll build our house." Accordingly, they designed it to make an easy transition to a pool room later on. Once the structure was complete, though, they were in for a surprise. "We discovered we don't really want a house," says Weisman. "At least not now, when we're working so hard. It's so nice to have such an easy place." (While he conceptualized the house, he turned to an architect friend, Richard Beard of the San Francisco firm of BAR, Inc., "to realize his vision for the property," as Beard describes it.)

Weisman jokingly describes the pavilion's style as "distilled Mediterranean." As in so many dwellings in that part of the world, it is wide open to nature. "The way the house frames the view is so axial and strong," he says, scanning the vineyard-lined valley with the Russian River in the distance. A generously wide pergola, lush with white wisteria and two kinds of grapes, runs the length of the pavilion; so, three steps down, does a fifty-foot pool, wide enough to accommodate a gang of visiting friends. When the French doors are open, both pergola and pool deck seem to dramatically extend the interior.

Of the house, Weisman says, "We wanted something very axial and symmetrical. We wanted it to have a little bit of grandeur, but definitely not be fancy." To this end, he and Fisher kept the scale

The pavilion "overlooks a valley of vineyards, the Russian River, and a really charming 1920s steel bridge," says owner Jeffry Weisman, who worked on its design with an old friend, Richard Beard of BAR, Inc., architects.

TOP LEFT AND BOTTOM LEFT: In the single room of his pool pavilion, Andrew Fisher transformed antique English chairs by adding a driftwood finish and leather cushions. The prints above the bed are antique engravings of insects. The Arts and Crafts bronze is in the style of Louis Comfort Tiffany.

TOP RIGHT: Fisher created the candlesticks on the mantelpiece from a pair of antique andirons and some black coral. The unusual bronze fireplace screen was made in New York. The carpet is an old Japanese tatami.

OPPOSITE PAGE: With its French doors opened, the terrace becomes an extension of the pavilion. The shell-encrusted Venetian-style lanterns, made by Fisher and Weisman, contain candles and are submerged in the pool.

large, with twelve-foot ceilings, but toned down the finishes, such as the limestone used for the fireplace, which was left unpolished. They stained the concrete floor themselves (so it would look "more like leather, very mottled and soft"), and used this same material on the terrace. The redwood ceilings were painted white for a warm, country look.

The house may be small, but it has a refinement of detail that is disproportionate to its size. "Everything has a little bit of a soft, low-keyed elegance," Weisman observes. Some of its pieces, such as the rare Venetian lamps by the bed, share a certain lightheartedness. Many were transformed by Fisher, who is also an artist. He rejuvenated the sleek antique English chairs (probably from the nineteenth century) with a driftwood finish and added exuberant pat-

terns to the bedside table, wryly described by Weisman as "in the manner of Cecil Beaton." As for the chandelier, "the two of us covered it completely in seashells and little mirrors," Weisman says. "It took over four months of weekends." An eighteenth-century French buffet separates living and sleeping areas.

So will there, one day, be a big house? "Perhaps later, toward retirement," Weisman answers. For now, he and Fisher love the minimal maintenance their pavilion requires. It has a way of welcoming guests, yet not encouraging them to linger. "In the summer we can have twelve seated for lunch under the pergola. We've even had a hundred. But then they all leave." The reason is obvious: "No guest room!"

THORNTON HOUSE

SONOMA, CALIFORNIA

Sometimes weekends and the houses they're played out in become one and the same. Such is the case with Laney and Anne Thornton's rammed earth house near the town of Sonoma, California, on which the couple worked for about six years. During this time, they stayed in another building on their more than three hundred acres, collaborating with the architects on every detail, beginning with the siting of the house and the installation of its lake. "Part of the weekend activity was building the house," Laney says.

The design, by Mark Kessler and Katherine Lambert of FACE Architecture and Design, a San Francisco firm, was inspired by a place beloved of the owners: an adobe house built centuries ago by General Vallejo, the nineteenth-century California military leader and state senator, on his ranch in nearby Petaluma. "He was Spanish and it was a Spanish-style house," says Thornton, who is chairman of the fashion company Eileen West. "It was made from the earth."

So is this place, which constantly refers to the marshland, savanna, and hills around it, with their indigenous trees and grasses. "I wanted a house that was about the setting, that was actually going to be made of local materials," Thornton says. Recycled redwood from demolished wineries was used for the rafters, among other areas;

bay trees that had fallen on the property were milled and crafted into cabinetry and floors. The earth for the walls, though, was brought in from elsewhere, according to Kessler, who notes, "Around here it's too clayey."

Rammed earth houses employ an ancient technique in which densely packed earth is used to create solid walls. Its technology was new to everyone on the team, which included contractor Herman Vojarsky, and they learned as they went. Varying wall textures throughout the structure document the group's ongoing experimentation with the material, a process they clearly enjoyed. "We really got into the geometry of the rammed earth and what you can do with it," Kessler says.

Modeled on a historical California residence, Laney and Anne Thornton's rammed earth house is set among vineyards, by the shore of a man-made lake. All the wood used in the house, from redwood to bay, comes from indigenous species.

TOP LEFT: Columns of rammed earth impart a rhythm to this view from the kitchen to the dining room via the main hall. Almost every column in the house shows evidence of experimentation with material and form.

BOTTOM RIGHT: "The house speaks to how it was built and what it was made of," says owner Laney Thornton. The master bedroom's outdoor shower area has redwood exterior walls — complete with bark.

OPPOSITE PAGE: The two-story central space, with its second-level arcade, is classic adobe. The rafters are of recycled lumber.

During construction, workshops were established in a large outbuilding on the property, including a forge and cabinetry and tile shops. Virtually every aspect of the house emerged from one of these, from the rammed earth walls themselves to the bark-covered exterior redwood columns. All counters, tiles, bathroom sinks, and scored slab floors, among other elements, were also made on site.

The architect describes this weekend place as "very basic, with rectilinear walls." As in General Vallejo's adobe, you enter a central, two-story area, with an arcade on the upper level. (Thanks to retractable skylights, this space literally opens up to the sky.) Every room can be reached via this central area: living, eating, and entertainment areas are downstairs; bedrooms upstairs. The large veranda,

on the house's south-facing side — also inspired by the Vallejo house — overlooks the lake and, in fine weather, affords a view of San Francisco in the distance ("It rises up almost like Florence," according to Thornton).

There are extensive gardens, including one containing a thousand roses, and twenty-six acres of vineyards. "I wanted it to be a house to have a bunch of people over for a day in the country. I made it an activity house," Thornton says, referring to its numerous fun structures designed for use by children, including a baseball diamond, batting cages, and trampolines. Most appealing of all is the trapeze-like contraption that allows you to zoom along a cable across the lake — definitely a temptation for adults, too.

OPPOSITE PAGE: "Wherever possible, the furniture is handmade in keeping with the house," Anne Thornton says. The woven leather Equipales furniture is from Mexico.

TOP LEFT: With its Equipales furniture and door made of nineteenth-century wine barrels, this corner of the master bedroom has a handcrafted feel.

BOTTOM RIGHT: In the master bedroom, as elsewhere, natural materials predominate. The palette here is tawny, almost woodsy, in keeping with the house.

TOP LEFT: Fissures in the rammed earth walls were deliberately kept evident. "They're kind of into the variations and cracks," architect Mark Kessler says of the house's owners. "They believe that something perfect is less than an asset."

BOTTOM RIGHT: The sink bowl, cabinet, and countertops in the master bathroom were all designed by the owners and architects and made on site.

OPPOSITE PAGE: A living room vignette. "It became like an altar," says Anne Thornton, who assembled these disparate objects, which include a traveling communion set that once belonged to her father, an Episcopal clergyman, and a Mexican good-luck charm.

129

ON THE COAST

Forget about voyaging to the ends of the earth. In a coastal house, you're already there. The land ends, the water begins, and you're left to contemplate a seascape that, while ever shifting, remains timeless. To spend time on the coast is to be constantly distracted; somewhere in the back of your mind, you're always aware of the sea.

For some of the houses in this section, from the Buckley family's Southern California beach house — a place designed to accommodate a large, extended family, a hefty percentage of whom are grown-up surfers — to Bo and Cathie Dahlstrom's crisp-lined house on Northern California's remote Lost Coast, the vista is the ocean. Other places here overlook such expansive bodies of water as a crystal-clear Canadian lake or the Long Island Sound.

There's a certain constancy to life at the water's edge. At the Grundys' beautifully restored house in Ontario, for example, summer ferries still crisscross Lake Rosseau, just as they have for more than a hundred years. As with so many coastal dwellings, this house seems to draw its very existence from its view. No matter how imposing the building, the water takes center stage. It's what draws you in, like a wave, in the first place, and it's what brings you endlessly back.

WESTPORT, CONNECTICUT.

130

DAHLSTROM HOUSE

SHELTER COVE, CALIFORNIA

It began with a newspaper ad for some "oceanfront property at a ridiculous price," as Cathie Dahlstrom, a child advocate, recalls it. Ridiculous, as in cheap. She and her husband, translator Bo Dahlstrom, who lived in San Francisco at the time, had wanted a weekend getaway for a long time. And the property, on the edge of the Pacific about two hundred miles north of the city, had exactly what they were after: beautiful light, fresh air, and, inescapably, the sea. "It was like Brigadoon," Cathie recalls, "so gorgeous we couldn't believe it."

Decades ago, when California's famous Highway 1 was being built along the Pacific — sometimes wedged into steep cliffs — only one stretch of land was so steep as to remain impenetrable, an area that has since been known, picturesquely, as the Lost Coast. "There's nowhere really much to hang a road here," Cathie says of this stretch of coastline, in the shadow of the King Mountain range. Since she and Bo wanted a place where their extended family could gather in nature, this remote area seemed exactly right.

As for the house itself, the couple looked no further than a compact cottage, built by a family friend named Charlie Barnett, in Marin County. "They liked my philosophy of making a small space look larger using scale," recalls Barnett, who had just finished architecture school at the time. The Dahlstroms bought the property and promptly gave the young architect his first commission: building their new house. (He now practices in San Francisco at Charlie Barnett Associates, which specializes in residential design.)

The couple's land sits nine hundred feet above sea level, overlooking the town of Shelter Cove and a twenty-four-mile stretch of lava beach. In every direction, there are amazing views, including "sunsets that are to die for," as Cathie describes them, not to mention the routine sighting of extraordinary things, from schools of dolphins to passing whales. Barnett knew right away that, because viewing is what this perch is all about, the house "had to be a takeoff on an old Coast Guard station." He studied books on such structures, then crafted one of his own. For their part, the Dahlstroms had just one requirement: that a tower be incorporated into the final design.

"Often I'll work with a vernacular on the outside, then, inside, things are a lot more modern, cleaner, more open," Barnett says. And so it is here: with its bright exterior — including a barn-red metal roof — the fourteen-hundred-square-foot dwelling is as efficient, yet full of personality, as a lighthouse; indoors, it's yachtlike in its compact craftsmanship. ("Tiny, but so together," as Cathie

"The way it's placed is so perfect, the way it perches on the hill," says Cathie Dahlstrom of her house near the King Mountain range on Northern California's Lost Coast.

Architect Charlie Barnett designed the house to resemble a Coast Guard tower. He toyed with scale, using French doors and high ceilings to make this small residence seem larger.

describes it.) To make it seem larger, the architect accentuated doors, windows, and ceiling heights and stuck to an open plan, with a kitchen that overlooks the living room. "We ended up with a lot of expandable areas," he says.

The house is designed to sleep a lot of people for its size, adds Cathie, whose tribe includes a grown daughter and some fifteen brothers and sisters (if you count step- and half-siblings). Barnett came up with some ingenious solutions to accommodate them all, including a sofa and chairs with built-in air mattresses and, in the master bedroom, a couple of under-the-bed storage spaces,

including one for storing tents. As a result, eleven people can sleep indoors comfortably; others — on one memorable occasion, an even dozen — stay outside in tents.

As for the interior, simplicity reigns. "Bo likes the starkness," Cathie says of her Finnish-born husband. "It's very Scandinavian. He likes things clean and fresh." But she also sees a more southerly influence at work. "Everything is so simple," she marvels, pointing out such high-tech details as steel strips between birch floorboards and cable beams stretched taut between living room walls. "It feels very Italian."

TOP: The master bedroom tower is so high that "the birds fly under you," owner Cathie Dahlstrom says. The built-in bed, with its under-bed storage, was designed by Barnett.

BOTTOM LEFT: The dining area, looking toward the kitchen. The ceiling tie-rods, deliberately exposed by architect Charlie Barnett, add drama and a high-tech feel. So do the birch plywood floors, which contain strips of stainless steel.

BOTTOM RIGHT: Designed for easy maintenance and located far from the beaten track, the Dahlstrom house is a perfect place to decompress.

GREENWOOD HOUSE

GALLIANO ISLAND, BRITISH COLUMBIA

"I wanted it as close to the water as it could go," says Barry Greenwood, of his eye-catching wood-framed house on tiny Galliano Island, in the Gulf Island chain off the western coast of Canada. Wedged between ocean and forest, his narrow, irregularly shaped half-acre site would have been a challenge for any architect. For Bo Helliwell, of Helliwell + Smith Blue Sky Architecture, a Vancouver firm he describes as "humane interpreters of the organic tradition of modernism," it was an irresistible one.

"Humane" is a good word in this context. Greenwood's retreat, which Helliwell has come to call "the Fishbones house," seems exactly that. It's a considerate structure, one that sits sinuously on the shoreline without seeming to disturb what owner Greenwood calls the "mind-boggling wildlife" that surrounds it. As for the organic part, Fishbones seems so much a part of nature that you half expect it to work its way loose from its foundations and wriggle into the sea.

The house resembles a fish on the inside, too. The ridgepole beam that runs through the structure acts as a kind of spine, with exposed cedar rafters extending from it like ribs. By varying the length of these rafters, the architects created the roof's dynamic shape. We "wanted to get the roof to have the same kind of flow as the shoreline," says Helliwell, who designed Fishbones with his wife and

business partner, Kim Smith. "We wanted to pick up on the natural sculpture of the land."

Greenwood, a Canadian, lived in Indonesia for a dozen years, working in the petroleum industry. He supervised the construction of Fishbones ("We spent almost two years fiddling, designing, getting it right.") while still residing abroad, with a view to retiring there with his wife, Sophia, and their two school-age sons. But, after his return to Canada, he ended up working in Vancouver instead and Fishbones became, temporarily, a weekend home.

With its picture windows and rows of skylights, this relatively compact structure seems larger than its three-thousand square feet. It is also exceptionally oriented to the outdoors. A window-lined gallery runs the length of the house, from front entrance to master

The house's serpentine lines recall the natural contours of the shoreline. "The roof flows like a wave," owner Barry Greenwood says.
To create its distinctive silhouette, architects Bo Helliwell and Kim Smith varied the lengths of its exposed cedar rafters.

bedroom, opening up onto the living and dining rooms. "When you're walking down the gallery it feels more like you're just walking along a path along the seaside," according to Helliwell.

The house is "a bit of East meets West," he adds. Its richly colored red cedar paneling may give it a Northwestern flavor, but its contents — including pieces from Indonesia, Korea, and Japan — definitely tug to the East. "Barry's wife is from Indonesia," the architect says, "and they bought quite a few artworks and artifacts over there that they wanted built into the house." While still in Asia, Greenwood made to-scale paper models of his furniture so that he could plot where each piece would go and edit his collection as needed. A privacy screen from Bali, incorporated into the hallway,

essentially became a carved piece of woodwork. The couple also had shoji screens built into the Japanese-style master bedroom, where they cover windows and doors.

If there is a decidedly nonweekend feel to the house, it's no accident; after Greenwood retires, the family will be ensconced in it full time. He ticks off the things he plans to do, including lots of gardening and time spent with his four children. And then there are the rewards of nature, as seen through the structure's panoramic windows. "There are eagles all over the place," Greenwood says, and, on one recent summer afternoon, "a super pod of over fifty killer whales" passed by. As he talks, you can almost hear him counting the days.

TOP LEFT: "There's a very conscious oriental influence in the house," architect Bo Helliwell says. In the entrance hall hand-colored trout etchings hang above an old Indonesian bench draped with antique Ikat cloth. The pillows are made from vintage sarongs from eastern Indonesia.

BOTTOM RIGHT: A window-lined gallery with exposed log rafters runs the length of this British Columbia house, affording a close-up view of the northern Pacific, with its exceptionally rich wildlife.

OPPOSITE PAGE: At sundown, the magic of this Pacific Northwest setting takes hold. Among the sights: otters and killer whales. "Sometimes, several pods of whales gather together for a summer party," the owner says.

OPPOSITE PAGE: The owner, a Japanophile, wanted a bedroom that entirely reflected that culture. The Mexican river rocks on the floor were lacquered and set in concrete to resemble the floors of Japanese bathhouses. Both the Meiji-period *tansu* chest and the ceramic hibachi date from the mid-nineteenth century.

"We usually work in a palette of native woods," architect Helliwell says. He and Kim Smith used architectural-grade red cedar wall paneling throughout; the floors and built-in cabinetry are cherry.

BUCKLEY BEACH COTTAGE

NEWPORT BEACH, CALIFORNIA

To spend time in Mimi and Peter Buckley's beach cottage is to feel you've entered the heart of Southern California. The sound of the ocean accompanies everything you do. The famous local boardwalk is just yards away, a magnet for what architect Laura Hartman calls "boardwalk culture" — nonstop rollerbladers, joggers, dog walkers, and the like.

With its surf shack, not to mention its surfboard kitchen counter, this twenty-five-hundred-square-foot, five-bedroom house speaks on every level of the beach. "It's a very appealing place for people who like big waves and want to get in the water," says Mimi Buckley, whose environmentalist husband, Peter, is a serious surfer. (She describes herself as "an architect, mother, and designer.") "It's very relaxed."

The 1940s-era bungalow-style cottage had been in her family for years. Eventually, she and her husband bought it from other family members, along with a property next door, and hired the Berkeley, California, firm of Fernau & Hartman Architects to bring it up to date. "It was a fairly humble and somewhat frumpy beach house," recalls Hartman, who, with partner Richard Fernau, had done several projects for the Buckleys in Northern California, where they

live. In an inventive renovation, the architects refocused the cottage, removing several previous additions to return it to its original structure. They redid the interior finishes and reoriented some bedrooms, adding a dormer window to one, so that each has an ocean view. New structures, including a guest house, surf shack, and garage (with a bunk room attached that's designed to sleep six children), were added and centered around a garden for a courtyard effect. They also added new framework to the hot tub — almost a necessity in this part of the world.

Here, as in their other projects, Fernau and Hartman were inspired by the Japanese tradition of *saki ori*, a technique in which patches, added to an original fabric, are made deliberately evident. Similarly, when these architects undertake a renovation, they try to make the scope of their additions clear. In this case, they varied the building

142

At the front gate, a view of the Buckley compound, including guest house and garden. As in so many houses by the architectural firm of Fernau & Hartman, the garden is an integral part of the design.

material for each part — using, for example, rustic redwood for the surf shack and cedar shingles for the main structure — so that "you can kind of see the intentionality to it," in Hartman's words. The neutral tones of the exterior walls are accented by bright pastel shades at the windows — what Hartman calls a "Diebenkorn palette," after the California artist.

Working with landscape architect Teresa Clark, the architects created a garden rich in tropical plantings — a living variation on the beach theme. "Almost all our residential projects have a garden at the center," says Fernau. "We design the inside and the out so that they're inextricably linked." The interior, too, speaks of the shore. Working with designer Marci Ellison, Mimi Buckley filled the house with vintage Hawaiian bamboo-caned furniture, much of it brightened by antique fabrics she picked up on the island of Kauai. Interspersed among these are some fun, attention-getting contemporary pieces, including a bright red couch by the Los Angeles furniture designer known as Harry.

The couple share their house with a steady stream of friends and relatives, and it seems to be in constant use. Amazingly for such a small structure, it sleeps seventeen. The architects designed it with visiting hordes in mind. "We wanted the house to be easy to use, legible," says Hartman. "It's very clear. You know where the dishes are." So, right away, do those who come here, drawn to a place where life really is a beach.

By filling the living room with vintage Hawaiian bamboo-caned furniture and bright contemporary pieces, owner Mimi Buckley and designer Marci Ellison brought the beach — and its culture — indoors.

OPPOSITE PAGE: A bedroom window overlooks the compound's other structures and one of Southern California's ubiquitous palms. By carefully manipulating the outdoor space, the architects made the site seem larger.

TOP LEFT: "We knocked a wall out between the living room and kitchen and put in a surfboard to act as a raised countertop and a visual division," Mimi Buckley says. The surfboard is by Greg Filtzer.

BOTTOM RIGHT: "We tried to use the spaces as efficiently as possible so lots of family could come," says Mimi Buckley. Here, one of its sleeping niches. The pillow fabric is Hawaiian.

NORDBERG HOUSE

SURREY, MAINE

One thing Marnee and David Nordberg knew for certain was that they didn't want a second residence. Absolutely not. "We always said we wouldn't have a vacation house," says Marnee Nordberg, an artist who lives with her radiologist husband just west of Boston. "It's too much work and we have too little time." Still, they reasoned, it couldn't hurt to look. The couple love Maine and — just for the fun of it, of course — began to look at houses in that state.

Then one day, a realtor led them to an open piece of land that slopes, very gently, down to a calm stretch of water known as Union River Bay. It was a clear day and you could discern the silhouette of Mt. Desert Island in the distance. From that point on, the couple's intentions were derailed. As for their architect, they first learned of Peter Forbes — who is based both in Italy and Boston — after an inventive, multipavilioned house he'd designed, also in Maine, was featured on the cover of a magazine. "We both felt very strongly about his sensibility," Nordberg reports. "It was us. We didn't look any further."

Light is a preoccupation of Forbes's (he describes one of his goals as "trying to capture light"), and it was what most impressed him when he visited the couple's land. "Their site is all about light. It's just a blaze of light. It's not the forest primeval. It's wide open field." It's also dangerously exposed. Not only is it a flood plain, but it faces the direction from which hurricanes blow. The challenge was to create a structure that, while using a lot of glass to take advantage of the views, could face down the elements. As for the clients, who have four children and numerous grandchildren, they wanted a place where they could house many guests, yet be assured of their own privacy. And Marnee needed space in which to create her abstract, yet landscape-based, paintings.

The elegant, thirty-two-hundred-square-foot house the architect devised — all pillars and glass — is ingeniously simple. "It's like a gazebo," Forbes says. "It's concrete posts with a roof." It is also a series of discrete, pavilionlike sections. One comprises the master bedroom, living room (known as the "great room" for its fifty-by-twenty-foot size), kitchen, and dining room; a guest area contains three bedrooms; and a third section, separated from the others by a short bridge, houses Marnee's atelier.

This Maine house is divided into three pavilions, creating a sense of privacy for each. "You have to go outside to get from one to the other," architect Peter Forbes says.

TOP RIGHT: View along the deck, facing south. The deck is counterweighted and built in segments; in stormy weather it can be folded up in front of the windows to protect the house.

BOTTOM LEFT: Forbes describes the house as "a prism for light." The side facing the Union River Bay is all glass. The roof is held up by concrete posts.

As for coping with the state's notoriously changeable weather, Forbes came up with a solution worthy of Jules Verne. "The deck is in segments between each pair of columns, and they swing up." Each deck is counterweighted and folds gently against the windows, shutting the house off from storms. How many other families, heading back to their weekday lives, have the luxury of knowing that their coastal home has been folded up securely into an impenetrable, origami-like box?

When the decks are down, life here is charged. "We have a constant house full of people," Nordberg explains; at any time, they might be scattered about the couple's four-and-a-half acres, boating, water skiing, or beachcombing for rocks, driftwood, and sea glass. In the evening, kids gather to play games in the living room. Yet this residence has an insouciant way with crowds. Even if a lively dinner is under way, each person can leave when the time suits: sleepy children can be carried to bed in the guest wing; the hosts can retire early to the master bedroom, which, separated from the living room by a stone fireplace, almost functions as a fourth pavilion. "We just bow out when we're ready," Nordberg says. And, after they do, the life of the house, in all its multigenerational diversity, goes on.

LEFT: By conceiving the house as predominately made of glass, Forbes opened it to light and views. "The water changes every minute," owner Marnee Nordberg says.

RIGHT: From a guest bedroom, a classic Maine waterscape. In clear weather, Mount Desert Island can be seen from the house.

A sitting room in the guest wing. The owners favor simple contemporary furniture, such as these pieces in rattan and leather. The large pots are from their extensive ceramics collection.

Forbes envisioned a "great room" for this couple's house, one that combines kitchen, dining, and living rooms. The master bedroom is on the other side of the fireplace.

OPPOSITE PAGE: A view from the "great room" to the kitchen gives a sense of the house's generous volumes. "Except for the guest wing, everything else goes up to the peak of the roof," the architect points out.

WORMSER BEACH COTTAGE

WESTPORT, CONNECTICUT

Almost every weekend, New York architect Peter Wormser, his wife, Liz Milwe, and their three small sons repeat the same routine. They drive to the Westport, Connecticut, town beach, park their car, toss weekend gear, groceries — perhaps even a child or two — into a cart, then haul it along to their hip-roofed, shingled beach cottage, which sits on a water-surrounded spit of land. "The winter is pretty intense," Wormser says. "To walk half a mile in the cold, carrying your things in a cart, it's not for everyone."

For this family, though, their cottage's isolation is very much part of its appeal. Built in 1910, it abuts the hundred-acre Sherwood Island State Park, overlooking the Long Island Sound on one side, a tidal marsh on another. "As you walk out here, every step you take is nature," says Milwe, who is a dancer and choreographer. Needless to say, this car-free area is an ideal place for the couple's bike-riding, rollerblading sons.

When Wormser and Milwe bought the twelve-hundred-fifty-square-foot structure about a decade ago, a lot of work needed to be done. Or, more accurately, undone. "It was an old summer beach cottage, but [its previous owners] had stripped away all its beachy quality," the architect recalls. "We put that back into the house." Wall-to-wall carpeting was removed and hardwood floors were added. Sheetrock was replaced by wainscoting and whitewashed wood "to give it the beach-cottagey feel that was at some point lost." Wormser adds that a lot of the work was extraction, describing how, in the master bedroom, he exposed wooden ceiling joists for a cathedral-like effect. (Now, the room feels satisfyingly volumetric.) Out on the porch, he transformed skinny columns — "little sticks," he calls them — into full-blown ones.

The couple kept the interiors simple to underscore the fact that, out here, it's nature that counts. Wicker chairs in bright colors enliven

The Wormser family beach cottage, looking out toward Cockenoe Island in the Long Island Sound. "Peter loves the garden part of it," his wife, Liz Milwe, says, recalling how he built this wall from stones found on the beach.

the living room, which overlooks Westport harbor. The rooms' relative sparseness plays up the art they contain. Many of the pieces on display, including a small but intense abstract painting above the living room sofa by New York artist Juan Ouslé, are by friends; others, such as Emmett Hitch's painting of a "dragon dog" in a child's bedroom, are drawn from the family's collection of outsider and folk art. The bright wooden masks over the fireplace were "done by myself and my children from remnants of housing I've been working on," Wormser reports. "It's recycled housing."

As for Milwe, "She responds to the house artistically in her own way," her husband says; at low tide recently, she choreographed and performed a new dance piece for a local audience on the sand flats in front of the house. Nature, too, has lately put on a well-received show. "The town is all excited because the osprey have returned," Wormser says. "It's a pretty special environmental spot."

TOP: Even in a child's bedroom, art is a focal point. The painting is by Leslie Alexander. Wormser replaced Sheetrock walls throughout the house with wainscoting and white-washed wood for a more beachy feel.

BOTTOM: On a child's chest of drawers is a casual mix of toys and art. The wooden sculpture was created by Wormser and his children.

Peter Wormser calls the house's interior "slightly colorful, but really very plain." In the living room, bright wicker furniture sets the tone. The painting is by Juan Ouslé, a Spanish painter now residing in New York.

OPPOSITE PAGE: At the end of a long day of play, the sun begins to set over the Long Island Sound.

GRUNDY HOUSE

LAKE ROSSEAU, ONTARIO

When Eric and Valerie Grundy leave their brick Tudor-style home in the center of Toronto each week, they do so in the time-honored way of so many weekenders: by car. But by the time the family, which includes three children, arrives at Ouno Island, just two hours north, they've traded one form of transportation for another. They finish their trip by powerboat, and their destination might as well be in another world.

Here, the seascape dominates. The Grundys' house looks out on the deep blue waters of Lake Rosseau, said to be the cleanest freshwater lake in Canada and one of three such bodies of water in the Lake Muskoka region. At the close of the nineteenth century, numerous wide-porched wooden structures were built around these lakes; known as "Olde Muskoka" homes, they're full of character and increasingly prized. Certainly they were by Eric, a clothing executive, and Valerie, a fundraiser. When house hunting they knew exactly what they wanted.

The Grundys' Olde Muskoka, which dates from 1898 and measures about forty-five hundred square feet, was once the island's main residence. (It has since been joined by half a dozen others.) Although a six-bedroom wing was removed more than twenty years ago, the structure still seems imposingly large. When the Grundys found it, the interior was still in excellent shape despite a century of weathering. But with its endless layers of paint and tumbling-down

outside stairways, the exterior was a different story. And the same was true for every outbuilding and dock on the four acres. "It took about three years to scrape every single inch of houses and boathouses down to the wood," Grundy reports. They also had the main house, which had become lopsided with age, raised and balanced, replaced every outdoor stairway, and converted an old canoe storage house into a gym.

Now the dwelling looks as pristine as the woodlands around it. It seems old yet new at the same time. And the same is true for the furniture it contains, much of which was already in the house. Although furnishing the place was as simple as a trip to the basement — "There was a hundred years of castaways down there," Grundy says — each piece had to be restored. The best of these, such as the wood table with yellow legs on the master bedroom's summer porch, share in the architecture's faintly otherworldly appeal. As for the rest, it was a question of filling in; although the

This nineteenth-century Olde Muskoka house is a classic of the genre; its close relations can be found in parts of Canada and across the northern United States, from Oregon to Maine. During its restoration, "we always tried to keep the character of the house," owner Eric Grundy reports.

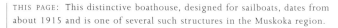

THIS PAGE: This distinctive boathouse, designed for sailboats, dates from about 1915 and is one of several such structures in the Muskoka region.

OPPOSITE PAGE: Canoe paddles and a vintage soda case sum up the essence of a Lake Rosseau summer. The darkest paddle (by the Orillia Canoe Company, from a nearby town of the same name) came with the house and dates from the time it was built.

porch's tall rocking chairs first rocked there just after the place was built, other pieces are new, including some wicker veranda chairs bought by the owners to match those that came with the house.

As the boathouses testify (including a wonderfully exotic-looking one — one of only three in the Muskoka region designed to shelter a sailboat), much of life here happens on the water's surface, in one sort of boat or another. In the evening, after a long day outdoors, the screened porches are where action of a rather more sedentary sort takes place. As Grundy describes it, "We 'assume the position,' which is what we call sitting on those rocking chairs"; like so many North Country residents before them, they rock through the long summer twilights, chatting and absorbing the beauty around them.

The family makes its way here every Thursday or Friday, from the time they open the house in April until they close it, just after the Canadian Thanksgiving, in October. Each time they pull up to their newly refurbished hundred-foot dock, Grundy says, he is awed by his own weekend dwelling. "We get off the boat and see the house, and it's perfect."

162

A fireplace setting in the children's bedroom — complete with a mounted deer head and vintage toys on the mantelpiece — captures this residence's rustic, unpretentious charm. The sign was created by the original owners.

TOP RIGHT: "If it's too hot inside, we sleep on the summer porch," Eric Grundy says. The sleeping porch off of the master bedroom was, in a way, a gift from friends; while staying in the house, they restored some furniture from its basement and arranged it in the space.

BOTTOM LEFT: "The house has such great bones," says owner Eric Grundy of his Ouno Island house. Here, its classic porch, where the owners "assume the position," as Grundy calls it, at the end of a long summer day.

BOTTOM RIGHT: Sunset over Lake Rosseau. Much of the furniture, both on the porch and throughout the house, dates from the house's early days and was restored by its new owners.

IN THE MOUNTAINS

"In the mountains, there you feel free . . ."

Mountains intoxicate. For those who thrive on snow-capped peaks and clear, high-altitude air, up high is, quite simply, the only place to be. For people who love peaks — and build houses among them — their appeal is many faceted. The high they induce, so to speak, doesn't come from anywhere else.

Sometimes, mountains are a state of mind. A couple of the following houses aren't truly at high altitude, but they offer a glimpse of distant peaks, and that can be mountain enough. Patrick Christopher's elegantly simple house by architect James Bischoff, at the foot of a seven-thousand-foot-high mesa, imparts a vivid sense of what it is to be down below when so much of your surroundings tower above. (For a break from canyon life, Christopher migrates skyward, to a cabin he owns on the mesa itself.)

Many who love the mountains are drawn to them for sports you can't do anyplace else. Skiing is a big draw for Al and Anita Waxman, who grab as much winter time as they can at their bright, audacious cabin in Aspen, Colorado, and for screenwriter Jamie Redford and his family, who spend a lot of their time in Sundance, Utah, on skis. But at least as alluring is the chance that mountains offer to enter a different world. Here, winter isn't a slushy inconvenience, but a celestially beautiful place in and of itself.

ASPEN, COLORADO.

166

BEATTIE HOMESTEAD

MCALLISTER, MONTANA

"It's the kind of house where, whenever you walk in, you see a different detail of workmanship," interior designer Diana Beattie says of the Double D Homestead, which she and her husband, Dick, a New York–based mergers and acquisitions lawyer, recently built near Bozeman, Montana. With its rustic exuberance, it is easy to see how its architect has come to call this "the three bears house." Set on two hundred acres of historic land (containing a once-active gold mine, among other intriguing relics), it's a place where craftsmanship has been taken to its absolute limit.

How the Beatties — quintessential easterners who have spent much of their lives in Washington, D.C., and New York — ended up in Montana is simple: they fell in love with the place. Dick, an avid fly fisherman, had kept a fishing cabin here for years. Inevitably, the couple soon wanted to spend more time in a state that Diana — only partly jokingly — calls "God's best work." Like the homesteaders who made their way out here a century ago, they set out to build a house.

The use of wood was inevitable. "Logs are what you build of around here," as Candace Tillotson-Miller, the couple's architect, says. "It just really is the Montana vocabulary." When word got out that Jane Fonda and Ted Turner, then still married, had put some old barns from their extensive Montana acreage up for sale, the Beatties bought three. "We ended up with these 1890 old log barns," says Diana, who also runs an events-planning business. "We used them as the footprint for our house."

The structures were dismantled, then reassembled at their site, which overlooks five ponds and is in listening distance of Washington Creek. "I had to do an infill connecting the three log buildings together," Tillotson-Miller explains. The largest barn became the main living area and kitchen; a traditional "dog-trot"–type building was used for bedrooms (including an enchanting space with a built-in, rustic bunk bed for the couple's grandchildren); a third structure was transformed into a horse barn. The finished building totals about three thousand square feet.

Both architect and clients credit some exceptional detail work by Harry Howard and his crew at the building firm of Yellowstone Traditions for the success of this project. "The most important thing about this site is the artistry of the craft," Diana says. "And that craft is carpentry."

The impetus behind much of the detailing was hers. "The house had a very strong masculine feeling," she says, "so I asked Harry to

"I felt very strongly that we do something traditional," the owner says. Architect Candace Tillotson-Miller crafted the house out of three old log structures, including a traditional "dog-trot" barn, using an infill to connect all three.

This chaise in the master bedroom of the Beattie homestead was made in New Hampshire in the nineteenth century. Its fabric, while loomed in Paris, has a Western motif. On the floor lies a cozy stack of five kilim rugs.

LEFT: "I think Montana is God's best work," says owner Diana Beattie. Here, sunrise over the Revenue Mountains.

RIGHT: The master bedroom is sited within earshot of Washington Creek. The mahogany four-poster bed is South American; the antique mirror is from the Black Forest. Beattie designed the chandelier, with its silver conchos, and had it made by Elkhorn Designs.

add wiggly wood, and other touches, to soften the feel. I wanted to add whimsy to the overall structure." Wiggly wood — a natural Western phenomenon that's just as curvy as it sounds — results when wormwood branches, in the course of a long Montana winter, become weighed down with snow. This unique material is used copiously here, from the fanciful porch railing to the ornate mudroom entrance. (Other elements, including carved doors inspired by Lech, the famous Austrian ski resort, and an upstairs bedroom that might have been lifted from an Alpine chalet, have decidedly non-Western origins.)

"We used old plaster and wonderful glazes to bring a warmth of color to the interior surfaces," Diana says. She furnished the place with local traditions in mind, using leather upholstery, for example, because it is a strong part of the Western vocabulary. The appearance of an occasional antique (such as the dining room's walnut hutch, from Normandy, which dates from about 1860) is also traditional, she explains: "Homesteaders coming out here would certainly bring a family heirloom." Because the couple's two grown daughters urged them to avoid hanging animal trophies, they have mounts on the wall that come from the Black Forest and from Indonesia, all made of wood.

The Beatties spend much of their time outdoors, hiking, fishing, riding, or just sitting on a meditation bench under a venerable Douglas fir. From here, they can keep tabs on the state's legendarily ever-changing weather and on moose and other animals in their native habitat. "You don't appreciate it back East, this utter peace," Diana muses. "Out here, I feel a far greater respect for nature."

TOP LEFT: In the "treetops" guest bedroom (added above the dog-trot barn) are an eighteenth-century French Normandy armoire and chest. The antique chaise longue — a mate to the one in the master bedroom — is covered in its original fabric.

TOP RIGHT: "The thing that makes this house special is the detail work," says owner Diana Beattie. This antler stair rail (by David Black, a local craftsman) includes fallen horn from moose, mountain sheep, and other animals.

BOTTOM: The guest bedroom painting is actually an oil-on-canvas fire screen, from the Colorado Mountains, dating from about 1820. The whimsically carved bed is contemporary Italian. The "lace leather" rocker is from Old Hickory.

OPPOSITE PAGE: Variations on a wooden theme, in the main cabin, looking toward the dining room. Even the trophy mount, which is Indonesian, is wood.

According to Beattie, there's a "fantastic cinemascope view into the valley" from these rustic, porch rocking chairs.

TOP: At the house's mudroom entry, architect Tillotson-Miller combined lodgepole pine, wood shingle, wiggly wood, and old logs. "There's a timeworn patina you don't get with newer logs," she says.

BOTTOM: "You don't have that appreciation of nature until you get out of the East Coast," says New Yorker Diana Beattie. Here, a view from the fishing cabin, looking toward Ward Peak.

REDFORD HOUSE

"My theory about our home, from the beginning, was the idea of utter simplicity," says Kyle Redford of the house she and her husband, Jamie, share on a mountainous stretch of land not far from Salt Lake City. "I wanted to focus on my family, rather than on the home. I didn't want to get there to find we'd further complicated our lives in a mountain setting."

Clearly, such worries were unnecessary. Life at the couple's family-centered, "kind of carpenter-built" cabin, as architect Howard Backen describes it, seems exceptionally serene, unless you count the occasional dramatic moment outdoors, such as when Jamie, a screenwriter, startled — and was startled by — a herd of elk during their migration a few seasons back. "They thundered into the woods, breaking trees and branches," he recalls.

The couple's twenty-five-hundred-square-foot house is located on what Jamie calls "family lands," a vast stretch of property that his father, actor Robert Redford, bought in stages, beginning in the 1960s. The land is now home to both a ski resort and the famous Sundance Institute, founded by the actor, which supports filmmakers and others in the arts and is the site of the annual film festival of the same name.

"My father always had the vision to create a family compound," Jamie says; years ago, the actor gave him and his two sisters property on which to build. Once they had children, Jamie and Kyle (who have a son and a daughter and live in Northern California) decided to break ground. "I just wanted it to be a place that could really withstand the wear and tear, hence the little furniture," says Kyle, a schoolteacher. "I wanted it to be well-edited and pleasing to the eye."

For its design, the couple turned to Backen, a Californian who has designed many of the "kind of humble, very livable, kind of taut" buildings, as he describes them, that typify the Sundance style. Working in the same vein, he created a straightforward wooden structure, one that, with its widespread porch, fits right in with the local vernacular. In contrast with many houses in this land of wide

"The idea was to do something small and manageable," owner Jamie Redford says of his house in Utah. Architect Howard Backen aimed for compatibility with the buildings of the nearby Sundance Institute, which he also designed.

179

open spaces, though, it feels relatively compact. "Jamie wanted a small house," the architect explains. "He feels comfortable in a tighter space." The floor plan is in a simple H-shape, with the living room where the letter's crossbar would be. One of the house's two adjoining wings is a two-story bedroom area; the other, which has only one floor, comprises a mudroom, entryway, and kitchen. A protected courtyard on the living room's southeastern side, complete with exterior fireplace, functions as an outdoor room.

With its almost sparse interior and copious wood paneling, the house has a Scandinavian feel. Kyle, who is of Swedish descent, had been attracted to the idea of curtained, wooden sleeping compartments since she first came upon them in *The Old Swedish Book*, a volume she loved as a child. (Backen built the compartments, as

well as the bedroom's armoires and other custom cabinetry.) The long wooden kitchen table, bought by the couple long before the house was built, is a perfect setting for the traditional Swedish dinner the Redfords host for friends and family each Christmas Eve.

The rest of the time, they share their property with a mixed crowd that includes brown bears, hawks, and mountain lions — more of them, happily, with every passing year. Once diminished by poisoned bait and overgrazing, this land is in the process of healing, according to Jamie, who adds, "It's one of the most uplifting things about being here. You have the sense of being in a place that's getting better and better."

180

TOP: In the living room, as throughout the house, simplicity is key. The stone fireplace repeats the one in the courtyard. The paneling is of western red cedar.

BOTTOM: In the Scandinavian-inspired kitchen, "We wanted a big long table where we could have lots of things going on at one time," Jamie Redford says. "People eating at one end, someone reading at the other."

OPPOSITE PAGE: With its wicker furniture and checked cotton fabrics, the master bedroom is simplicity itself. The boxes on the end table are Shaker.

TOP: In the children's room, the curtained sleeping compartments provide "a little privacy within a not-so-private room," Kyle Redford says. They were built by the architect, based on an idea Kyle recalled from childhood.

RIGHT: A hammock — and its young occupant — define the edge of the porch. Landscaping was kept to a minimum, at Jamie's request. "I wanted the wild grasses to grow up to the porch, uninterrupted," he says.

WAXMAN HOUSE

ASPEN, COLORADO

"It's a party house," says Al Waxman of the playful, eye-catchingly bright habitat to which he and his wife, Anita, retreat among the peaks of Aspen, Colorado. "We love color." You could hardly fail to notice. The living room alone is alive with it: yellow conical lights, bright stained glass, brilliantly hued geometric carpets. The kitchen dazzles. The color palette in the master bathroom might have been inspired by a bag of M&Ms. "This is a couple that enjoys aggressive design," says architect James Biber, who also did the interior design.

Fearless, too. Enormous faux apples, bright red and made of polyurethane foam, dangling from cottonwood trees in front of the house set the humorous, almost Disneyesque tone. Even something so ordinarily tame as a carpet in the master bedroom "is almost like a psychedelic version of a stone floor," according to Biber, a New York–based principal with the multidisciplinary design partnership known as Pentagram.

Biber admits to having "turned up the volume" for these avid art-collecting clients, for whom he once designed a multicolored loft in New York's SoHo. "It was really a reaction to what I know about the owners. I recognized at what level they like to have the intensity of their finishes." Their Aspen home, which they share with their children, is a haven from New York, where Al works as an entrepreneur

and venture capitalist and Anita as a theater producer. "In the summer, people rotate through the house," Al reports.

The couple came to Colorado for the usual reason: nonstop, high-altitude beauty. "Aspen brought us out there," Al explains. "The sound of Maroon Creek caused us to buy the house. You can hear it all the time." Wedged in a canyon on a four-acre plot at the edge of a national forest, its views are some of the most famous in the Rockies, from Pyramid Peak to the much-photographed mountain vista known as Maroon Bells.

Once upon a time, when this six-thousand-square-foot residence belonged to the actress Ann-Margret, it was a very conservative house, according to Biber, who describes it as "clapboard, slightly

The morning frost burns off to reveal another perfect Rocky Mountain day. Owners Al and Anita Waxman joke that the seductive sounds of Maroon Creek, which runs by the house, "forced" them to buy their house.

Victorian." In what he calls a "pretty radical renovation," he transformed it, aiming for a log cabin feeling both inside and out. He added pine logs to the exterior walls and, on the inside, replaced plaster and Sheetrock with timber. Most dramatically, he created a twenty-two-foot-tall central space, containing both a dining room and staircase, with a double-story window and enormous stone fireplace. Before, the house "sat with this spectacular view to the south, but didn't open up to it," Biber says. Now, "with this big vertical slot of glass you really see the view from the mountaintops to the water about a hundred feet below."

The house's handcrafted feel is due to numerous local craftspeople — metalworkers, forgers, glass artists, cabinetmakers, and the like — who filled it with their workmanship; the hand-hammered leaf-pattern staircase rail, for example, was made by a local blacksmith. As for the interior design, "our whole approach is to get a lot of art," Al says. This they did, using some of the same whimsical art by some of the same artists as in their city home, including pieces by such exuberant contemporary masters as Kenny Scharf and Red Grooms. Throughout, they had a simple goal, he adds: "To make it unboring." Consider it done.

"It was simple to make it dramatic," says architect James Biber of the dining room. "We tried to create a big central space, with a staircase, that opens up to the view." The iron-and-wood stair rail was done by local craftsmen.

OPPOSITE PAGE: "It sits right in this vertical slot," Biber says of the house, which is located in a canyon. Oversized apples of polyurethane foam, by a local artist, sum up the owners' playful approach.

TOP LEFT: In the living room are a spherical brass low table by New York artist Carmen Spira, yellow conical lights, and a bright wool rug inspired by paving stones. The custom carpet is by Christine Vanderhurd.

TOP RIGHT: In the kitchen, "the faucets and the toaster are the only things not custom made," Biber jokes. Both this room and the bright bathroom, which are contained in a two-story tower on the corner of the house, are new.

BOTTOM: Although it seems neon bright, this couple's Rocky Mountain house has "a much more earthy feel than our New York loft," says owner Al Waxman.

OPPOSITE PAGE: The Disneyesque bathroom includes a strategically positioned rubber duck. The console, with its round counter and bright drawers, by architect James Biber, was his "way to insert lots and lots of color into the room."

CHRISTOPHER HOUSE

It feels like you've arrived at the very end of America. Deep in a canyon in southeastern Utah, at the end of a rough, meandering road — one that crisscrosses the same creek three times over and is hence called Los Vados, or the crossings — a metallic-roofed house sits unassumingly on the land. In this "canyon country setting," as the owner calls it, with huge, brilliantly colored mesas looming overhead, this structure, intelligently enough, doesn't choose to compete with nature. Realistically, nothing could.

In the face of such riotous beauty, "it was our intent to make the house as simple as we could," says architect James Bischoff, using an adjective that comes up often when he and client Patrick Christopher, a restoration architect, talk about this retreat. "Patrick is very much into simplicity. He didn't want to make a replica of an older building. He wanted it to have timeless lines," adds Bischoff, who has studied in Athens and has a deep appreciation of classic forms.

Although both Bischoff and Christopher flirted with the idea of doing a rustic cabin or an adobe-style dwelling, in the end they opted for "a traditional simple building," as the architect describes it. He calls this solar-powered house "classic in its way. It's all tripartite themes and very geometric." But don't expect Ionic

columns and marble. Instead, the structure is simplicity itself, from its materials (board-on-board walls, masonry columns, a corrugated metal roof) to its floor plan.

At the heart of the house — which Christopher shares with his partner, Gary Denmark, an abstract painter — is what Bischoff calls "the fireplace room," a living room equivalent, with the master bedroom on one side, kitchen on the other (a second bedroom is tucked into a back corner behind the kitchen). "It's tiny, about eight hundred square feet," he notes. "But certain things about it feel kind of grand. The ceilings are ten feet high."

The large rock balanced on the chimney top, among other touches, comes straight from Western tradition. "Very often stones were put

"The whole plan is classical and very geometric," architect James Bischoff says of this desert house near Moab, Utah. "It was our intention to make it as simple as we could."

OPPOSITE PAGE: The porch at night is a place of warmth and shelter. Canvas shades pull down for protection against the wind. The acrylic-on-wood painting above the fireplace is *Bedouin*, by resident artist Gary Denmark.

on top of chimneys to keep out the rain," Bischoff explains, adding that "I always wanted to stick a big stone on top of a chimney. It's just such a traditional reference and it's totally not the way tract houses do things." Neither is the generous two-level veranda to which visitors gravitate in order to enjoy the house's views — and soundtrack. "It's really oriented to the creek," Christopher says. "You hear the water all around you. For a desert setting, that's marvelous."

With its African masks and textiles (combined with some of Denmark's bright abstract paintings), the interior reflects years of travel and adventure. "I wanted to do something in the desert that kind of pulled together more of the experience of safari," says Christopher. "The only thing missing is the large animals." The

tawny earth tones within the cabin also reflect the surrounding landscape.

Like the British in colonial India, who headed up into the hill country each year to avoid the suffocating heat, the owners often retreat to a "very simple summer-use shack" that Christopher restored, one that's at a safe remove from the hundred-plus temperatures of the canyon floor. "We use it as a place to cool off," he says of this dwelling, which is perched on a seven-thousand-foot mesa. From this vantage point, you feel on top of the world. "You can watch the weather coming from miles away," Christopher observes, adding, with deep understatement, "It's a good alternative to urban life."

OPPOSITE PAGE: "Going into the desert has been an incredible experience," says painter Gary Denmark, whose studio in the mesa house is shown here. "Working abstractly, I still get so much of my information from my surroundings."

TOP LEFT: The client "wanted the house close to the creek so you could hear that sound in the desert," the architect says of the canyon house. The water runs year round — a rarity in southern Utah.

BOTTOM RIGHT: In Christopher's mesa house, the furnishings are less spare, the palette higher toned. A 1950s Mexican wool blanket hangs from the sleeping loft. The small area rug is Navajo, the quilt, American.

TOP: Breakfast, mesa style. Beyond a bowl of bleached bones, scavenged from around the house — the unforgettable Utah landscape.

BOTTOM: The porch of the mesa house affords a bird's-eye view of this corner of southern Utah. The mountain bike is indispensable for exploring the mesa, which runs for several miles. A Navajo blanket hangs over the rail.

OPPOSITE PAGE: Christopher and Denmark use their mesa house — which sits at seven thousand feet — as a place to cool off in the desert's scorching summer heat.

SOURCE LIST

CANADA

British Columbia

Inform Interiors Inc. Contemporary furniture, lighting, home accessories from Canada and all over the world. Also has a design-related book department. 97 Water Street, Vancouver, B.C. V6B 1A1. (604) 682-3868.

Ontario

Quasi Modo. Furniture ranging from contemporary to vintage, with a distinct modernist edge. Also, work by contemporary Canadian designers. 789 Queen Street West, Toronto, Ontario M6J 1G1. (416) 703-8300.

Roots Home. Home furnishings, accessories, linens, traditional cabin furniture. 195 Avenue Road, Toronto, Ontario M5R 2J3. (416) 927-8585.

UNITED STATES

California

LOS ANGELES
Algabar. Asian and European furniture, both antique and contemporary. Exotic gifts. 920 N. La Cienega Boulevard, Los Angeles CA 90069. (310) 360-3500. www.algabar.com

Country Floors Inc. 8735 Melrose Avenue, Los Angeles, CA 90069. (310) 657-0510. Ceramic and stone tiles from all over the world, some antique, some new. (Also in New York City at (212) 627-8300.)

Kathryn Ireland. Wonderful fabrics, many hand silkscreened. Also, lampshades, slipcovers, couches, country French ceramics. 1118 Montana Avenue, Santa Monica, CA 90403. (310) 393-0670.

Liz's Antique Hardware. Vintage hardware from 1820 to 1960. Will match old pieces. Also has contemporary line. 453 South La Brea, Los Angeles, CA 90036. (323) 939-4403. www.lahardware.com

Modern Living. Contemporary Italian designer furniture. 8775 Beverly Boulevard, Los Angeles, CA 90048. (310) 657-8775.

Outside. Vintage patio furniture. Restored one-of-a-kind pieces from the 1940s to 1960s. Also some contemporary. 442 North La Brea, Los Angeles, CA 90036. (323) 934-1254.

Room with a View. Home accessories, linens, bath, ceramics, much of it European. 1600 Montana Avenue, Santa Monica, CA 90403. (310) 998-5858.

Soolip Bungalow. Home furnishings, fabrics, and furniture with an Asian bent. Chinese antiques; contemporary furniture by California designers. 548 Norwich Drive, West Hollywood, CA 90048. (310) 360-1512.

SAN FRANCISCO BAY AREA
Coquelicot. Artisan-made items from Provence. Ceramics and linens are exclusive to the shop. 503 Magnolia Avenue, Larkspur, CA 94939. (415) 924-0279.

Forrest Jones, Inc. One-of-a-kind ceramic lamps made on the premises. Also, china, baskets, linen, ceramics, and home accessories, both imported and domestic. 3274 Sacramento Street, San Francisco, CA 94115. (415) 567-2483.

Limn. Contemporary furnishings and accessories from Europe and the U.S. Also, customized Bulthaup kitchens from Germany. 290 Townsend Street, San Francisco, CA 94107. (415) 543-5466.

Nest. A newer variation of the San Francisco store of the same name, this one specializing in French rustic furniture, decorative objects, quilts, linens. 340 Presidio Avenue, San Francisco, CA 94115. (415) 776-7289.

Sue Fisher King. Home furnishings, linens, tabletop, decorative accessories, gifts. 3067 Sacramento Street, San Francisco, CA 94115. (415) 922-7276.

Yeni Home Furnishings. Asian furniture, art, and accessories, both contemporary and antique, including bronzes, porcelain teapots, antique baskets. 1309 Howard Street, San Francisco, CA. (415) 255-0502.

SANTA BARBARA
Upstairs at Pierre Lafond. One-of-a-kind items, both old and new, including bedding made of antique damask, pewter, handblown glass, and antiques from Turkey, Japan, and elsewhere. 516 San Ysidro Road, Montecito, CA 93108. (805) 565-1503.

William Laman Furniture-Garden-Antiques. Informal antiques from Europe and Asia, home furnishings, accessories. 1496 East Valley Road, Montecito, CA 93108. (805) 969-2840.

Colorado

Cry Baby Ranch. Everything for the Western home, from dining tables to frames. 1422 Larimer, Denver, CO 80202. (303) 623-3979.

Crystal Farm. Manufacturer of antler chandeliers and furniture. 18 Antelope Road, Redstone, CO 81623. (970) 963-2350.

Connecticut

West Country Antiques. French and English antique country armoires, farm tables, and other furnishings. 334 Washington Road, Woodbury, CT 06798. (203) 263-5741.

Florida

Arangoto. Contemporary design, from furniture to tableware, much of it from Europe. 7519 Dadeland Mall, Miami, FL 33156. (305) 661-4229. www.arango-design.com

Luminaire. European contemporary and modern design and accessories; also, design-related books. 2331 Ponce de Leon Boulevard, Coral Gables, FL 33134. (305) 448-7367. (Also in Chicago at (312) 664-9582.) www.luminaire.com

Hawaii

Ets'ko. Furniture and gifts from around the world, especially Asia, including *tansu* (Japanese chests), screens, porcelain, Italian glassware, some modern furniture. 35 Waianuenue Avenue, Hilo, HI 96720. (808) 961-3778.

Illinois

A New Leaf Studio and Garden. Whimsical, handcrafted accessories, pottery, and furniture from such countries as Mexico and the Philippines. Also, exotic plants, including orchids. 1818 North Wells, Chicago, IL 60614. (312) 642-8553.

Michael FitzSimmons Decorative Arts. Furniture, lighting, ceramics, textiles. Specialists in the American and British Arts & Crafts movement. 311 West Superior Street, Chicago, IL 60610. (312) 787-0496. www.fitzdecarts.com

Pavilion Antiques. Eclectic French furniture and accessories. Also, garden furniture, mirrors, lighting, industrial design. 2055 North Damen Avenue, Chicago, IL 60647. (773) 645-0924.

Richard Norton, Inc. at Country House. Eighteenth- and nineteenth-century French and English furniture and accessories. 179 East Deerpath, Lake Forest, IL 60645. (847) 234-0244.

Maine

Apples. Country decorative accessories, many in the form of animals, such as wooden roosters. Also, pottery, linens. (Note: this is a seasonal store, open only in July and August.) 103 Babbidge Road, Islesboro, ME 04848. (207) 734-9727.

Massachusetts

La Ruche. Rustic chandeliers, lamps and lampshades, embroidered tablecloths from France, needlepoint pillows, Italian mohair throws. Hand-painted furniture by local artists. 168 Newbury Street, Boston, MA 02116. (617) 536-6366.

Leonards New England. Seventeenth- and eighteenth-century beds, armoires, dressers and other furniture. Some reproductions. Will resize antique beds. 600 Taunton Avenue, Seekonk, MA 02771. (508) 336-8585.

Michigan

Marco Polo. Painted American country and provincial European furniture. Handcrafted accessories, rugs, textiles. P.O. Box 331, 13630 Red Arrow Highway, Harbert, MI 49115. (616) 469-6272.

Missouri

Centro. Contemporary furniture and lighting by noted European architects and designers. 4729 McPherson Avenue, St. Louis, MO 63108. (314) 454-0111.

Montana

Antler Designs. Horn chandeliers, trophy mounts, rustic and hickory furniture, antler lamps with rawhide shades. 119 East Main Street, P.O. Box 928, Ennis, MT 59729. (406) 682-4999, (800) 522-0999.

Davis-Torres Collections. Large selection of rustic furniture made from old wood. 14 West Main Street, Bozeman, MT 59715. (406) 587-1587.

New Mexico

Dewey Galleries Ltd. Native American artifacts, tin work by Maurice Dixon, New Mexican antiques, some contemporary furniture. 53 Old Santa Fe Trail, Santa Fe, NM 87501. (505) 982-8632.

Faircloth/Adams. Antique fabrics, mainly American. Also, folk art, quilts, furnishings. Hotel Loretto, 211 Old Santa Fe Trail, Santa Fe, NM 87501. (505) 982-8700.

Nomad's. Textiles, antique furniture and pottery, handwoven wool carpets, chiefly from Morocco. 207 Shelby Street, Santa Fe, NM 87501. (505) 986-0855.

New York

NEW YORK CITY
Craft Caravan Inc. African handicrafts, including furniture, sculpture, and textiles. 63 Greene Street, New York, NY 10012. (212) 431-6669.

Galileo. Classic modern furniture, some vintage, some new, and accessories from all over the world, from jacquard tablecloths to Murano glass. 37 Seventh Avenue, New York, NY 10011. (212) 243-1629.

Howard Kaplan Antiques. Eighteenth- and nineteenth-century French and English antiques. 827 Broadway, New York, NY 10003. (212) 674-1000.

Interieurs. Exclusive architect-designed contemporary furniture line. Also carries French and Asian antiques. 114 Wooster Street, New York, NY 10012. (212) 343-0800.

Jacques Carcanagues, Inc. Furniture, textiles, and decorative objects from Southeast Asia, Burma, India, Thailand, and the Philippines. 106 Spring Street, New York, NY 10012. (212) 925-8110.

Kevin Hart & Co. Antique and new furniture, lighting, home accessories from France, the Far East, Morocco, and elsewhere. 31 N. Moore Street, New York, NY 10013. (212) 966-1963.

Liz O'Brien. Twentieth-century decorative arts including furniture, carpets, lighting, objects. 800A Fifth Avenue, New York, NY 10021. (212) 755-3800.

Moss. Furniture, housewares, and decorative objects by leading designers and architects. 146-150 Greene Street, New York, NY 10012. (212) 226-2190.

Niall Smith Antiques. Neoclassical furniture and objects, including some Biedermeier. 344 Bleecker Street, New York, NY 10014. (212) 255-0660. Also at 96 Grand Street, New York, NY 10013. (212) 941-7354.

Nomad Rugs. Tribal kilims, saumaks, and piles from Central Asia, both new and antique. 470A Broome Street (entrance on Greene), New York, NY 10013. (212) 941-7352. Also at 95 Crosby Street, New York, NY 10012. (212) 219-3330.

Portantina. Decorative objects from all over, including cushions, glasses, coasters, candleholders. Also, Venetian velvet, sold by the yard. 895 Madison (at 72nd Street), New York, NY 10021. (212) 472-0636.

William Lipton Ltd. Early Chinese furniture and related works of art. 27 E. 61st Street, New York, NY 10021. (212) 751-8131.

LONG ISLAND
Bagley Home. Rural farm-style painted furniture, new Amish tables, kitchen antiques, old French country linens, pillows, ironstone pottery. 155 Main Street, Sag Harbor, NY 11963. (516) 725-3553.

Zeff. Eclectic furnishings and accessories, many of them imported. Recent finds: a wainscoted day bed; Moroccan carpets; African lamps. 46 Jobs Lane, Southampton, NY 11968. (516) 283-2999.

UPSTATE
Rural Residence. Items from Hudson Valley designers, including china, glassware, linens, antiques. 316 Warren Street, Hudson, NY 12534. (518) 822-9259. www.ruralresidence.com

Theron Ware Antiques. Formal and country European and American antiques. Specialists in mirrors and in garden furniture and statuary. 548 Warren Street, Hudson, NY 12534. (518) 828-9744.

Pennsylvania

Owen Patrick Gallery. Avant-garde home furnishings. 4345 Main Street, Philadelphia, PA 19127. (215) 482-9395.

Weisshouse. European and American contemporary and classic furniture. 324 South Highland Avenue, Pittsburgh, PA 15206. (800) 422-7848. For more casual, eclectic furniture and home accessories: Weisshouse Design Store. 5511 Walnut Street, Pittsburgh, PA 15232. (412) 687-1111.

South Carolina

152 A.D. Architectural elements, garden furniture, painted mirrors, handmade accessories. 65 Broad Street, Charleston, SC 29401. (843) 577-7042.

Texas

Surroundings. Furniture, accessories, textiles from Central and South America and around the world. 1710 Sunset Boulevard, Houston, TX 77005. (713) 527-9838.

Washington

Current. Very contemporary furnishings, chiefly from European designers. Also, lighting and a full line of Danish wood stoves, known as *rais*. 629 Western Avenue, Seattle, WA 98104. (206) 622-2433.

Wyoming

Elkhorn Designs. Western chandeliers, antler lighting fixtures, mirrors, and furniture, much of it incorporating unusual materials, such as hide, iron, and mica. P.O. Box 7663, 165 N. Center Street, Jackson, WY 83002. (307) 733-4655. www.elkhorndesigns.com

Fighting Bear Antiques. Early Arts & Crafts, Mission, and Old Hickory-style furniture. Also, pieces by western designer Thomas Molesworth. P.O. Box 3790, 35 East Simpson, Jackson, WY 83001. (307) 733-2669.

The following is a list of designers and architects whose work is featured in this book:

Anderson Architects, p.c.

55 Vandam Street
New York, NY 10013
Tel.: (212) 620-0996
Fax: (212) 620-5299
E-mail:
info@andersonarch.com
Ross Anderson

Architects Santa Fe

466 West San Francisco Street
Santa Fe, NM 87501
Tel.: (505) 983-5497
Fax: (505) 983-4078
E-mail: asf1@concentric.net
Jake Rodriguez

Howard Backen

Backen Gillam Architects
1028 Main Street
St. Helena, CA 94574
Tel.: (707) 967-1920
Fax: (707) 967-1924
Sausalito office:
(415) 289-3860
E-mail: diana@bgarch.com

Pamela Banker Associates

136 East 57th Street
New York, NY 10022
Tel.: (212) 308-5030
Fax: (212) 308-5032
Pamela Banker
E-mail: pbdecor@aol.com

**BAR, Inc.
Architecture, Planning,
and Interior Design**

1660 Bush Street
San Francisco, CA 94109
Tel.: (415) 441-4771
Fax: (415) 536-2275
Web: www.BARArch.com
Richard Beard

**Charlie Barnett
Associates**

626 Hampshire Street
San Francisco, CA 94110
Tel.: (415) 824-0478
Fax: (415) 824-0462
E-mail: cbarnett@charliebar-
nettassoc.com
Charlie Barnett

Diana Beattie Interiors

1136 Fifth Avenue
New York, NY 10128
Tel.: (212) 722-6226
Fax: (212) 722-6229
In Montana:
Tel.: (406) 682-5700
Fax: (406) 682-5701

James Bischoff

49 Alcatraz
Belvedere, CA 94920
(415) 435-8492

Mario Buatta

120 East 80th Street
New York, NY 10021
(212) 988-6811

**Carter LaRoche Interior
Design**

181 Winslow Way, suite F
Bainbridge Island, WA
98110
(206) 842-2089
Trina LaRoche

Patrick Christopher

Restoration Architect
120 Alpine Terrace
San Francisco, CA 94117
E-mail:
rpchrist@ix.netcom.com

**FACE Architecture and
Design**

69 Clementina Street
San Francisco, CA 94105
Tel.: (415) 957-0961
Fax: (415) 957-1380
E-mail: mark@face.clrs.com
Mark Kessler
Katherine Lambert

**Fernau & Hartman
Architects**

2512 Ninth Street, #2
Berkeley, CA 94710
Tel.: (510) 848-4480
Fax: (510) 848-4532
E-mail:
general@fernauhartman.com
Richard Fernau
Laura Hartman

Field Paoli Architects

1045 Sansome Street
San Francisco, CA 94111
Tel.: (415) 788-6606
Fax: (415) 788-6650
E-mail: jlf@fieldpaoli.com
John Field

**Fisher Weisman Design &
Decoration**

616 Minna Street
San Francisco, CA 94103
Tel.: (415) 255-2254
Fax: (415) 255-1254
www.fisherweisman.com
Andrew Fisher
Jeffry Weisman

**Peter Forbes and
Associates, Architects**

70 Long Wharf
Boston, MA 02110
Tel.: (617) 523-5800
Fax: (617) 523-5810
Peter Forbes

Peter Gilliam
**John Wheatman &
Associates, Inc.**

1933 Union Street
San Francisco, CA 94123
Tel.: (415) 346-8300
Fax: (415) 771-8652

Global Possibilities

1250 6th Street, Suite 402
Santa Monica, CA 90401
Tel.: (310) 656-1970
Fax: (310) 656-1959
E-mail:
casey@globalpossibilities.org
Casey Danson

Louis Goodman

M. Louis Goodman Architect
181 Waverly Place, #4F
New York, NY 10014
Tel./Fax: (212) 645-2682

**Helliwell + Smith Blue
Sky Architecture**

4090 Bayridge Avenue
West Vancouver, B.C. V7V
3K1 Canada
Tel.: (604) 921-8646
Fax: (604) 921-0755
E-mail: blue.sky@pro.net
www.blueskyarchitecture.com
Bo Helliwell
Kim Smith

Marc LaRoche Architects

181 Winslow Way, suite F
Bainbridge Island, WA
98110
Tel.: (206) 842-1366
Fax: (206) 842-1394

San Francisco Office:
1736 Stockton Street
San Francisco, CA 94133
Tel.: (415) 399-9229
Fax: (415) 399-1764
E-mail: mlrarch@serv.net

Ricardo Legorreta

Legorreta Arquitectos
Palacio de Versalles 285-A
11020 Mexico City, D.F.
Mexico
Tel.: (52) 5-251-9698
Fax: (52) 5-596-6192
E-mail:
legorreta@data.net.mx
Ricardo Legorreta
Victor Legorreta

Lori O'Kane Design

1028 Main Street
St. Helena, CA 94574
Tel.: (707) 967-1925
Lori O'Kane Backen

Patkau Architects, Inc.

560 Beatty Street, suite L110
Vancouver, BC V6B 2L3
Canada
Tel.: (604) 683-7633
Fax: (604) 683-7634
E-mail: general@patkau.ca
John Patkau
Patricia Patkau

Pentagram Architecture

204 Fifth Avenue
New York, NY 10010
Tel.: (212) 683-7071
Fax.: (212) 532-0181
E-mail:
architecture@pentagram.com
James Biber

David Salmela
Salmela Architect

852 Grandview Avenue
Duluth, MI 55812
Tel.: (218) 724-7517
Fax: (218) 728-6805
E-mail: DDSalmela@aol.com

Berta Shapiro Interior
Design

225 West Huron, suite 214
Chicago, IL 60610
Tel.: (312) 951-7464
Fax: (312) 951-7465
Berta Shapiro

Candace Tillotson-Miller

P.O. Box 467
Highway 10 West #862
Livingston, MT 59047
Tel.: (406) 222-7057
Fax: (406) 222-7372
E-mail: milleraia@mcn.net

Wagner Van Dam Design
& Decoration

853 Broadway
New York, NY 10003
Tel.: (212) 674-3070
Fax: (212) 995-9861
E-mail:
timothyvandam@wagner-
vandam.com
ronaldwagner@wagnervan-
dam.com
Ronald Wagner
Timothy Van Dam

Walker/Warner
Architects, Inc.

835 Terry Francois Boulevard
San Francisco, CA 94107
Tel.: (415) 626-6632
Fax: (415) 626-6858
E-mail: bwalker@walker-
warner.com
Brooks Walker III

Wormser + Associates,
Architects

644 Broadway
New York, NY 10012
Tel.: (212) 505-6962
Fax: (212) 477-0273
E-mail:
wormseraia@aol.com
Peter Wormser

Yellowstone Traditions

P.O. Box 1933
Bozeman, MT 59771
Tel.: (406) 587-0968
Fax: (406) 586-2999
E-mail: harry@yellowstone-
traditions.com
Harry Howard

Mark Zeff Consulting
Group

260 West 72nd Street,
suite 12B
New York, NY 10023
Tel.: (212) 580-7090
Fax: (212) 580-7181
E-mail: mzeff@idt.net
Mark Zeff

ACKNOWLEDGMENTS

A thousand thank yous to the following, who helped this project in so many different, generous ways:

Rutgers Barclay

Marisa Bartolucci

Jim Brosseau

Baynard Chanler

Rosalie and Bill Chanler

Colleen Daly

Martin Filler

Diana Fuller

Sandra Gary

Lucy Gray

Kari and Gordon Holmes

Dennis Hult

Alan Jolis

Diana Ketcham

Ann Landi

Shirley and Irving Loube

Linda Mack

Byron Meyer

Craig Miller

Susan Miller

Sherry Morse

Elizabeth Plater-Zyberg

Barbara Plumb

Ted Pugh

Margaret and John Robson

Eliot Rowlands

Amy Schireson

Radek Skrivanek

Anne Sprecher

Susie Tompkins

Pilar Viladas

Esther Wanning

Michael Wollaeger

Penny Wollin

Clelia Zacharias

And to our agent, Fred Hill, for his canny guidance; to Nion McEvoy, Leslie Jonath, Christina Wilson, and David Becker at Chronicle Books, for their humor and encouragement; an enormous thank you to Suzanne Darley for her super styling skills and consistent support; to the entire Loube family, both in California and in Canada; and to Julian Rowlands, for last-minute editorial assistance; above all, salaams and salutations to the myriad weekenders whose houses are shown in these pages. Thank you for your endless time and patience and for so cheerfully sharing your end-of-the-week houses, lives, and stories with us.

~ PENELOPE ROWLANDS
AND MARK DARLEY

INDEX